A Full Employment
Program for the 1970s

edited by
Alan Gartner
William Lynch, Jr.
Frank Riessman

A Full Employment Program for the 1970s

PRAEGER SPECIAL STUDIES IN U.S. ECONOMIC, SOCIAL, AND POLITICAL ISSUES

Praeger Publishers   New York   Washington   London

Library of Congress Cataloging in Publication Data
Main entry under title:

A Full employment program for the 1970s.

    (Praeger special studies in U.S. economic, social,
and political issues)
    Bibliography: p.
    1. United States—Full employment policies—Addresses,
essays, lectures. I. Gartner, Alan. II. Lynch, William,
1941-   III. Riessman, Frank, 1924-
HC106.6F84   331.1'1'0973   75-36408
ISBN 0-275-22810-X
ISBN 0-275-89560-2 student ed.

PRAEGER PUBLISHERS
111 Fourth Avenue, New York, N.Y. 10003, U.S.A.

Published in the United States of America in 1976
by Praeger Publishers, Inc.

In memory of our friends,
George A. Wiley
Russell A. Nixon
Both fighters for justice and equality.

Page

As unemployment levels grow higher and higher, the need for a serious full employment program becomes clearer. When we use the term full employment we mean, unequivocally, the end of involuntary unemployment. In such an economy everyone who wishes to work is guaranteed the opportunity to do so—for a decent wage and under decent conditions. While the authors of these essays may have differences about various aspects of implementation (for example, macroeconomic planning rather than large-scale public service employment), they are united regarding the need to make a full employment program an immediate operational priority.

Never since the enactment of the 1946 Employment Act (not, as it is often mislabeled, the Full Employment Act, a quite different piece of legislation which was not enacted but which had an advanced progressive focus) has unemployment fallen below 2 percent, and only in the overheated Korean and Vietnam War economies has it been below 4 percent. These rates, however, record a distorted picture of the actual situation: only those persons who have expressed their willingness and ability to work by actively and unsuccessfully seeking it, during the four weeks previous to the enumeration, are counted as unemployed. Those too discouraged to seek work, those who work part-time but who would work full-time if such employment were available, those stuck in training programs but who would prefer to be working, those who have joined the armed forces for lack of work in civilian life, and those left uncounted because the enumerators' sample found them underrepresented are not included in official unemployment estimates.

When, for example, the "official" unemployment rate was 7 percent in 1971, Gross and Moses calculated that the "real" unemployment rate (those included in the official count plus those "disclosed but set aside" and those "hidden and ignored" was closer to 25 percent.[1] If these ratios held at today's "official" rates, the actual unemployment would be close to one-third of the real labor force!

Even this staggering figure is not fully descriptive. As an overall figure, it does not show the rates for the various subgroups of the population. The present 9 percent (official) unemployment has to be doubled to describe official black unemployment, and among black teenagers the official rate is over 40 percent. The 9 percent unemployment rate also means that more than 8.5 million persons are unemployed at a given moment and that some 25 million persons are unemployed at some time over the course of the year. But the burdens are spreading. During 1975, 52 percent of the nation's families were directly affected by unemployment: 30 percent because some family member had been laid off, 9 percent because they had lost overtime, and 13 percent because their work week had been cut back. Of the married men unemployed 59 percent had wives who were either unemployed as well or who were not in the labor force. Adding in the families headed by women who ordinarily worked but were now unemployed, and subtracting the families in which there was a wage earner other than the family head, 70 percent of the families with head-of-household unemployed had no member holding down a job.[2]

Nine percent official unemployment means immense suffering among millions of individuals: suicide rates soar, mental hospital admissions rise dramatically, and crime rates increase as the fabric of social life is threatened by the absence of what is crucial in our work-ethic culture—jobs. It means great cost to government too—an estimated $16 billion in lost revenues ($2 billion for unemployment insurance, plus other funds to maintain the unemployed, and $14 billion in taxes) for every 1 percent increase in the unemployment rate.* A wide variety of income surrogates or supplements have been added to unemployment insurance: expanded food stamps, free breakfast and supper programs, clothing stamps, transportation stamps, payment of health insurance for the formerly employed, as well as loans to defer mortgage payments, and, of course, welfare rolls continue to grow.

All of this reflects and reinforces an exceedingly costly shortfall in goods and services not produced.

During 1953-74 inclusive, actual total national production measured in 1970 dollars was more than $2.1 trillion below what it would have been had full employment been sustained in a full economy during those 22 years.[3]

This is a peculiar way to run a society: millions of people who want to work cannot; much needed goods and services, public and private, are not provided in education, health, safety, transportation, housing, museums, parks, and libraries. But leading decision makers in business and in politics prefer to hold to their belief in the benefits of unemployment, still reminding us as Business Week did more than 20 years ago that "There's no assurance against inflation like a pool of genuine unemployment."[4] AFL-CIO President George Meany made the same analysis when he charged that the Ford administration prefers high unemployment because it keeps labor weak and wages down and it "disciplines the work force."[5]

---

*Increases in unemployment insurance represent the largest domestic increase in the 1976 federal budget.

Traditional Keynesians argue that by tuning the economy carefully, unemployment can be effectively held down, but as we have suggested above and as Killingsworth notes in this volume, "creeping prosperity unemployment" is not simply a function of inadequate "aggregate demand," rather, it grows out of the very structure of the United States' economy. A part of the issue is the high productivity of agriculture and some sectors of industry (particularly the production of military goods) using capital-intensive technology and complex systems of organization and management. Simply, fewer and fewer people are needed to produce more and more of some goods. (We shall discuss below some of the costs of this.) Further, as many have noted (see Killingsworth and Harrison in this collection), the structure of American labor markets is not unitary. Some talk of a "dual labor market," while others put forth the notion of as many as five labor markets. The point is that overall increases in aggregate demand do not have the same effect upon each labor market. For, as Ulmer points out, in the recession years of 1958 and 1961, "the unemployment rate for professional and technical workers was at 2.0 percent; for managers and administrators in those years, it was 1.7 and 1.8 percent respectively." But, for the economy as a whole, it was over 7 percent, with 10 percent for semiskilled operatives, and 15 percent for unskilled nonfarm laborers. Conversely, in the boom years of 1966 and 1969, when overall unemployment was at 4 percent or below (and at 1.0 percent or less for professional and technical workers and managers and administrators) the rate for operatives never fell below 4 percent and it remained between 6.5 and 7.5 percent for nonfarm laborers.[6] What this means, in effect, is that within an overall policy there must be carefully targeted planning of specific policies for particular goals.

The deficient performance of the economy, reflected most clearly in the failure to achieve full employment, has not, then, been borne equally. To improve the performance of the economy so that greater income equity and job access can be obtained would suggest the need for policies and programs which will require national economic planning for the United States. Recently planning has attracted increased attention from businessmen and labor leaders, a prestigious committee cochaired by a Harvard, Nobel Prize-winning economist and the UAW's president, and has prompted bills proposed by both Republican and Democratic senators. Such widespread support must and does mean that the idea of "planning" has different meanings for its varied proponents. For some, it is a way to rationalize management of the economy in order to assure the stability deemed prerequisite to sustained high levels of profit. For others, it is a device to get a better "handle" on what is happening in the country with the expectation that knowing more will allow the nation's leaders to guide it better. And, for yet others, it is seen as a step toward an economy increasingly managed by the public, a step which may be down the path toward socialism.[7]

For us, planning is a tool in the struggle to achieve a just society. The redistributive effect of full employment is a key aspect of that effort as well as an immediate amelioration of critical hardships. A full employment program has redistributive effects both in terms of the income derived from the jobs it generates, as well as in the services provided through the public service employment which would necessarily be a part of a full employment program. These services are redistributive both in terms of their intrinsic value (what S. M. Miller has called "the new income,") and also in the instrumental function they play, particularly for the poor in providing access to other benefits.[8]

So far, it has only been in periods of maximum military expenditure when this country has come closest to full employment. This is a dead-end street—demanding periodic reversals in job stability, and threatening to both local resources and world peace. Remember that military expenditures are particularly inflationary as the incomes paid to defense workers add to aggregate demand without generating a concurrent increase in the supply of goods and services available for purchase. Recall also that military expenditures are both capital-intensive and earth resource-depleting; and both capital and earth resources are in limited supply. It is only in allocating a sizeable portion of an escalating military budget, and refashioning a tax system, that the resources necessary for full employment can be marshalled.

We are not talking about growth versus no growth; rather we are interested in the kind of growth we enjoy in this nation—who pays for it and who benefits. Arthur and Stephanie Pearl have suggested that the quality of life enjoyed in an ecologically sound, full employment, human-service society would represent a dramatic improvement.[9] Indeed, Sweden, Denmark, and Switzerland, all have a higher gross national product (GNP) per capita than does the United States, despite a use of energy around half per capita that in the United States, or less. Unfortunately, in the United States, we continue to rely heavily on the energy-producing industries that comprise the most capital-intensive and least labor-intensive sector of the economy. "Accordingly, each dollar of investment capital taken out of energy production and invested in something else, and each personal-consumption dollar saved by reduced energy use and spent elsewhere in the economy will create more jobs than are lost."[10]

Such a society is not cost-free. It will not come about, as some in the 1960s appeared to have hoped, simply as a consequence of growth. It will not come about without cost. The costs must be borne by the many powerful individuals who benefit from unemployment, who profit from sectors of the economy that are particularly capital-intensive, and for whom the tax system provides shelters, loopholes, and intergenerational transfers of wealth and power, as well as by those whose well-being is the consequence of racism and sexism. Clearly, some specific measures are necessary—price and profit controls, a revamped taxation system, credit allocation for public good, and most probably increased public ownership. However, not public ownership of the kind Robert Lekachman calls "citrus nationalization" (that is, nationalization of industrial "lemons") but public ownership and/or control of key sectors of the economy, along with public determination of policies in other sectors.

Full employment is the key to a healthy economy and viable society. Whether one believes, as we do, that the ultimate resolution will involve substantial public control (an American version of democratic socialism) or, if one prefers the system basically as it is, without full employment, the strains will become so great that less democratic social control mechanisms become necessary.

NOTES

1. Bertram Gross and Stanley Moses, "Measuring the Real Work Force: 25 Million Unemployed," Social Policy 3, no. 3 (1972): 5-10.

2. Harris Poll and Department of Labor Survey quoted by Eileen Shanahan, "The Mystery of the Great Calm of the Unemployed," New York Times, 3 August 1975.

3. Leon Keyserling, Full Employment Without Inflation (Washington, D.C.: Conference on Economic Progress, 1975), p. 9.

4. Business Week, 17 May 1952.

5. George Meany (An address before the Full Employment Action Council, Washington, D.C., June 17, 1975).

6. Melville J. Ulmer, "Full Employment Without Inflation," Social Policy 5, no. 5 (January/February 1975): 10.

7. For a discussion of these and other alternatives, as well as a report on planning in Western Europe and Japan, see a series begun in Social Policy 5, no. 6 (May/June 1975).

8. On this point, see Colin Greer, "Introduction," in Alan Gartner and Frank Riessman, The Service Society and the Consumer Vanguard (New York: Harper & Row, 1974).

9. Arthur Pearl and Stephanie Pearl, "Strategies for Radical Social Change: Toward an Ecological Theory of Value," Social Policy 2, no. 1 (May/June 1971).

10. John P. Holdren, "Too Much Energy, Too Soon," New York Times, 23 July 1975.

1

THE HISTORICAL BACKGROUND OF FULL EMPLOYMENT POLICY

Russell A. Nixon

THE GUARANTEED FULL EMPLOYMENT GOAL

The guarantee by a government of full employment, of guaranteed employment for everyone able and willing to work, represents
a social, political, and economic policy fundamentally different from
even the most eager and progressive interventionist approach to minimizing unemployment. It posits full employment as a first and irre-
ducible commitment. It is founded on a definition of "full employment" that reduces involuntary lack of work to temporary and
frictional factors.

In his June 1944 report, Full Employment in a Free Society,
Sir William Beveridge defined full employment as meaning "having
always more vacant jobs than unemployed men [sic], not slightly
fewer jobs. It means that the jobs are at fair wages, of such a kind,
and so located that the unemployed men [sic] can reasonably be expected to take them; it means, by consequence that the normal lag
between losing one job and finding another will be very short. . . .
Those who lose jobs must be able to find new jobs at fair wages within their capacity, without delay."[1]

In the epochal 1949 United Nations report by "A Group of Experts" on National and International Measures For Full Employment,
"the practical meaning of Full Employment" is defined as "a situation

Originally published in Public Service Employment: An Analysis
of Its History, Problems, and Prospects, Alan Gartner, Russell Nixon,
Frank Riessman, eds., (New York: Praeger Publishers, 1973), pp. 11-
27, 223-25. © 1973 by Praeger Publishers.

in which there are no unemployed persons . . . a situation in which unemployment does not exceed the minimum allowances that must be made for the effects of frictional and seasonal factors."[2]

In practical terms two concrete situations of full employment are illustrative. In the United States during the five years of World War II the equivalent of 25 million full-time workers moved into employment (military or civilian), raising the labor force from 45 million to 70 million. The anticipated labor force growth during 1940-45 was exceeded in actuality by almost 8 million. The overall labor force participation rate rose from 56 percent of the noninstitutional population to over 63 percent in 1944. Unemployment was officially reported as 1.2 percent for 1944. For the short-term at least, there was full employment.[3]

The Soviet Union represents a second concrete example of full employment. As reported in a paper prepared by the U.S. Department of Commerce for the Economic Committee of NATO in June 1971 on ''Manpower Trends in the USSR: 1950 to 1980'': ''During the 1960's a steadily increasing number of newspaper articles, scholarly papers, and official documents published in the Soviet Union noted the existence of a labor shortage throughout the Soviet Economy. Many of these publications contained warnings that the shortage would continue throughout the 1970's and have serious effects on the growth of the economy, and there is ample evidence to support this thesis. . . .''[4]

Obviously there are basically different routes to full employment in a socialist planned economy and in a capitalist free enterprise system. The UN experts emphasized in their 1949 report to the secretary general the point of view that there is a ''compatibility of full employment with the essential principles of any economic system. . . . The full employment pledge does not impose upon any country the obligation of altering the basic features of its economic system. . . .'' The experts noted that:

> In countries in which there is a considerable degree of central direction of the economic system, the mechanism of planning and control can be used to ensure that all available labour is in fact employed. In countries which rely primarily on the system of private enterprise, concern is sometimes expressed lest a policy of full employment may entail the introduction of controls of a type considered foreign to their economic institutions. In our view, however, the steps required to promote full employment in free enterprise economies are fully consistent with the institutions of such countries.[5]

Without pursuing the matter at length, there is a presumption that the planned economy can maintain full employment easily, even that it is a condition inherent in a fully planned system. In a basically unplanned economy, of which the United States is a major example, full employment would seem to involve a combination of strategies such as those outlined earlier as relevant to seeking high employment. The distinguishing feature between the high and full employment strategies may well include different degrees of fiscal and monetary intervention. But most particularly job creation shifts from minimization of unemployment to an open-ended program whose size is determined simply by the size of the job gap unfilled by the stimulated private economy. In a sense, and even though there are good grounds for opposing the reference as demeaning to public employment, job creation through planned public works and public service employment becomes a "last resort" strategy aimed at meeting the residual employment need that remains after the private sector has "done its best."

There are important and expanding varied conceptions of full employment going beyond the definitions cited and having major policy implications. They represent increased sophistication and higher standards, which reflect advanced social and economic perceptions and enhance and extend the full employment goal, making it more and more difficult to achieve. They also reflect different time and structural change dimensions. The phases of this progressing conception of full employment are more or less as follows.

Jobs for All—Everybody Has an Opportunity to Work

The central point of this conception is that no person able and willing to work lacks a job. Jobs may be make-work jobs, and a type of sheltered workshop approach may assure that no one need be idle. At one extreme this situation can be represented statistically in much the same terms as our current official estimates of unemployment— that is, everyone actively seeking work who works even one hour in the survey week is classified as employed, and everyone who does not find at least one hour's work is deemed unemployed; considerations of pay, conditions, and duration of work are not taken into account. The quantitative measure may expand to include involuntary part-time work, but this concept is essentially quantitative without regard to the quality of employment.

A Good Job at a Living Wage for All

In this concept the ante is raised—full employment is seen as requiring a certain quality in the jobs provided, which eliminates involuntary part-time work and pays a living wage with good working conditions. This conforms with the Universal Declaration of Human Rights adopted by the United Nations General Assembly on December 10, 1948, which provides as "the common standard of achievement for all peoples and all nations . . . the right to work, to free choice of employment, to just and favorable conditions of work and protection against unemployment" and a living wage. This standard is reflected in the special U.S. Labor Department subemployment index based on a survey in 13 slum areas in 1966, which included involuntary part-time employment, subpoverty level wages, and the "discouraged workers" not counted in the labor force.

Jobs for All with Decent Pay and Conditions and Realistic Opportunities for Upward Mobility and Work at Full Capacity

A very major dimension is added to the concept of unemployment and full employment when underutilization of the current actual and the potential capacity of the labor force is considered. The quantity of human resources unused due to lack of opportunity is not quantifiable, but it is undoubtedly an unemployment factor of great importance. It has been emphasized by the impact of the civil rights, manpower, and antipoverty movements in the 1960s, with their attention to upward mobility, upgrading, and career advancement. The new work opportunities for the disadvantaged, the New Careers programs with job restructuring and the reduction of artificial credentials barriers, and the provision of new support and remedial services are all directed toward this aspect of unemployment.

Full Employment that Means Full Development and Full Utilization of the Total Voluntary Potential of Human Resources Over Time

The ultimate in full employment is achieved when adequate training, rehabilitation, and labor market structural adjustments are combined with overall demand for labor, which provide jobs and careers for all able and desiring to work. This is a full employment dimension rarely achieved, and it is enhanced as more time is allotted to the pro-

cess. This conception involves time to overcome handicaps of all sorts
of disabilities—physical, mental, and social. It includes adjustments
in work schedules, such as increased part-time and flexible work hour
arrangements, as well as facilitating transportation, location, etc. As
the ultimate full employment dimension, anyone not working in this
model has essentially chosen leisure over increased income.

Clearly the differences and the different policy implications of
varying full employment models are very important. Essentially what
is required is unlimited demand pressing on limited labor resources,
with the magnet of opportunity constantly pulling on each person as he
chooses to work and to expend the efforts necessary to advance occu-
pationally in return for differential rewards. The assumption is that
each individual has free choice whether to work and to advance.

The development of the conception and the realization of full
employment over time and in varied situations reflect these different
perceptions of what full employment means.

THE CONCEPT OF FULL EMPLOYMENT—BEFORE WORLD WAR II

Unemployment has been the subject of economic and social concern since the earliest days of mercantilism in the fifteenth century.
Until the twentieth century, relief of the unemployed poor consisted of
either direct "outdoor relief" or the workhouse, with encouragement
of the economic growth of the factory system as the ultimate solution.[6]
While the general antagonism to idleness may have represented a
back-handed concept of full employment there was no such general
concept in effect.

The idea of assuring jobs for all was an idea, as Michael
Harrington has commented, "that has been loitering in the corridors
of socialist thought for at least 145 years. Louis Blanc, a French
historian and, briefly, a government official, first formulated the concept of governmentally guaranteed work in 1836. It was tried in Paris
during the Revolution of 1848 and, until the philosophical ascendance
of Marxism in the last quarter of the 19th Century, it was what most
Europeans understood to be socialism."[7]

Full employment was assumed to be an inherent feature of Uto-
pian socialist plans. For example, in Edward Bellamy's Looking
Backward—2000-1887, Dr. Leete told Julian West that in the old system "It eventually happened then (1887) that vast numbers who desired to labor could find no opportunity" but that now "the principle
of universal military service, as it was understood in (1887) . . . is
simply applied to the labor question."

This, Dr. Leete explained in the Bellamy fantasy, was
something which followed as a matter of course as soon
as the nation had become the sole capitalist. The people
were already accustomed to the idea that the obligation
of every citizen, not physically disabled, to contribute
his military services to the defense of the nation was
equal and absolute. That it was equally the duty of every
citizen to contribute his quota of industrial or intellectual
services to the maintenance of the nation was equally
evident, though it was not until the nation became the
employer of labor that citizens were able to render this
sort of service with any pretense either of universality
or equity.[8]

In his analysis of capitalism, Marx developed the thesis that the
system has a chronic incapacity to achieve full employment and that
the creation of "a reserve army of the unemployed" was an inherent
feature of the system. On the other extreme the classical economists
denied the possibility of serious continuing unemployment in the competitive free enterprise system. Thus in Alfred Marshall's Principles
of Economics, the classic statement in 1890, unemployment or "in-
constancy of employment" is mentioned in less than 10 of the book's
858 pages. Unemployment was only an accidental aberration, as the
system maintained the essentially optimal level of employment on almost an automatic basis.[9] Later, in 1909, the eminent economist
H. Stanley Jevons wrote on "The Causes of Unemployment" and made
the point that the "unemployable" and the unemployed are really identical. The causes of unemployment were (1) the inefficiency of the
education system which produced unemployable children, (2) the trade
unions that pushed wages too high, and (3) trade fluctuations related
to "Solar Activity" affecting the sun's heat.[10]

Gradually economists began to recognize that all unemployment
was not simply frictional, and they gave their attention to technological, trade cycle, and monetarily caused unemployment. But these were
almost "by the way" observations that persisted until the Great Depression. As Schumpeter suggests, the "indictment stands against the
vast majority of the economists of that period . . . with few exceptions,
of which Marx was the most influential one, they treated cycles [read
unemployment] as a phenomenon that is superimposed upon the normal
course of capitalist life and mostly as a pathological one; it never oc-
cured to the majority to look to business cycles for material with
which to build the fundamental theory of capitalist reality."[11]

The Great Depression forced a revolution in the way of thinking
and acting about unemployment. That story has been told many times
and need not be repeated here. Pragmatic considerations led to large-

scale job creations, with relief and preservation of the system as the primary objectives. In his first inaugural address, on March 4, 1933, President Franklin D. Roosevelt said "Our greatest primary task is to put people to work." In his second "Fireside Chat," on September 30, 1934, Roosevelt said, "I stand or fall by my refusal to accept as a necessary condition of our future a permanent army of unemployed. On the contrary, we must make it a national principle that we will not tolerate a large army of unemployed. . . ." This obvious emphasis had no need for any sophisticated or well-developed concept of full employment: the totally unemployed are estimated officially to have been 25 percent of the labor force in 1933, and the official National Resources Committee (NRC) estimated that on the basis of "full time equivalents" unemployment averaged 45 percent of the total available labor supply for 1932, 1933, and 1934.[12] It should be noted that the NRC data prepared by David Weintraub, then director of the WPA National Research Project on Reemployment Opportunities and Recent Changes in Industrial Techniques, approximately doubled the unemployed labor force estimates indicated by the official Census Bureau data.

The conceptual approach to unemployment was revolutionized in 1936 by the appearance of John Maynard Keynes' seminal volume, The General Theory of Employment, Interest and Money.[13] Keynes destroyed the Walras-Marshall laissez-faire equilibrium approach to full employment and built the theoretical and analytical case for government intervention to affect the levels of employment/unemployment. Economists and public officials of the New Deal eagerly grasped Keynes' General Theory as the bible guiding activist interventions to reduce unemployment. With unemployment in the 15-30 percent range, liberals and even radicals marked themselves in "Keynes clothing" as they advocated strong government actions for "full employment," both to meet the continuing Depression crisis and then to prepare for defense and wartime production.[14]

Although the left was attracted to Keynes' advocacy of government intervention against unemployment, the Keynes theory was not a full employment theory. It essentially gave a theoretical foundation to and even justified a stabilized level of "acceptable unemployment." Although originally embraced primarily by liberals, Keynesism is essentially a conservative "state capitalist" approach to the economy and to unemployed resources. This is exemplified by a statement of President Richard M. Nixon's: "I am a Keynesian." Given the real political economy of capitalism that is the frame of Keynes' analysis, conservative Keynesism is the real Keynesism. Keynes has given us a theory of unemployment, not a theory of full employment. Keynes sets the stage for, and makes viable in a managed way, a concept of spurious full employment. Lacking a rigorous conceptualization of

what full use of labor resources means, the way is open for the game
of debating whether an official unemployment rate of 2, 3, 4, or 5 percent is "full employment." Moreover the long and devious process
of statistically manipulating official unemployment data so as to minimize the publicly acknowledged gap between actual and potential labor
power utilization is perfectly compatible with the spurious full employment concept.[15]

Various expressions of full employment did begin to appear after
Keynes' General Theory. The often cited An Economic Program for
American Democracy published by seven young Harvard and Tufts
Keynesian economists in 1938 spoke vaguely of "eradicating unem-
ployment."[16] In 1939 one of the leading liberal New Deal economists,
Mordecai Ezekiel, wrote a polemic for democratic economic planning
that he titled Jobs For All: Through Industrial Expansion. The author
warned:

> Democracy is doubly challenged. Communism on the one
> side, and fascism on the other, both proclaim that they are
> the way to full employment and opportunity for the com-
> mon man . . . we must solve our own problem of unem-
> ployment. We must reopen the doors of opportunity for all
> our growing youth and our displaced middle-aged. . . .
> There should be a stirring call to press forward now for
> a full-bodied War on Poverty. We should center our na-
> tional effort now on expanding production and doing away
> with unemployment and poverty. . . .[17]

A pioneering and more precise conception of "practical full
employment" was developed by the National Resources Committee
in its efforts to quantify the "Loss in Potential Real National Income
Due To Depression Unemployment of Men and Machines, 1930-37."
Using WPA labor force estimates it was assumed that a "residual unemployment" of about 3.7 percent of the total labor force actually
represented "practical full employment" in 1938.[18] As the beginning
of World War II drew near, the vague approach to full employment
began to merge from concern about economic recovery to potential
war mobilization. Even conservative sources sought to debunk the
size of the published estimates of unemployment needing public attention. New Deal economists were being called upon to estimate how
much unused labor might be realized for the very practical "full employment" of war. Even the most expansive estimates were soon to
be surpassed by reality, as World War II moved the country from
massive unemployment in 1939 to at least full and perhaps "over-
full" employment in 1944.

BEFORE WORLD WAR II: JOB CREATION
TOWARDS FULL EMPLOYMENT?

Precise data about the labor force, employment, and unemployment during World War I are not available. Although U.S. involvement
actively covered only 20 months of the war, from April 6, 1917 to
November 11, 1918, military personnel on active duty rose from just
under 180,000 in 1916 to almost 2,900,000 in 1918. There was considerable expansion of war work, and the inflow of the anticipated
500,000 immigrants was suddenly ended. Together these factors
created a tight labor market, with the reported result that "the actual
shortage in man power was in effect the most significant economic
shortage in the war."[19] But the problem was satisfactorily met by a
system of labor exchanges, some special training efforts, the beginnings of "dilution of skilled labor," and a system of labor priorities
that "guided the flow of labor from less essential to more essential
industries and to prevent the very wasteful rapid turnover which war
conditions engendered. . . ." But the chairman of the War Industries
Board, Bernard M. Baruch, was able to successfully oppose the drafting of labor as unnecessary "given the country's large reservoir of
labor."[20] Full employment was not achieved, and a serious general
labor shortage was not a problem in World War I.

In practical terms full employment was never an issue during
the Great Depression and the New Deal. The economic breakdown
was so massive that all concrete programs were aimed simply—and
totally inadequately—at reducing the 15-25 percent overall jobless
level. Even limited goals of "acceptable unemployment" and "high
employment" were never really within reach, let alone aiming at the
prospect of any of the four "full employment" models mentioned
earlier. As late as 1940 the official unemployment rate was about
15 percent. As summarized by Arthur E. Burns and Edward A.
Williams, "Since 1935 the total number given employment on various
public work programs has ranged from a low of 2.3 million to a high
of 4.6 million. Large as these figures are, at the peak they represented less than half of the number estimated as unemployed. Indeed,
throughout this period these programs have averaged only between
one-quarter and one-third of the estimated unemployed."[21]

The relevance of the New Deal experience was practical, not
conceptual, insofar as full employment was concerned. It was demonstrated that large-scale government intervention through both public
works and direct public employment is a viable and effective way to
create jobs and reduce the volume of unused human resources.

As the Great Depression led to large-scale unemployment and
attendant destitution, "emergency" became the prime factor in the

development of public programs. In the initial stage of the Depression, 1930-32, the central issue was transfer of traditional state and local relief responsibility to the federal government. For a while in this period contradictory programs developed as many states and localities cut down on such usual public services as schools, hospitals, sanitation, and police in order to divert funds to relief.

The history of the development of work-relief programs from 1930 to 1940 is one of experimentation and improvisation. One program led to another revised program reflecting the previous experience. The sequence moves from the early state and local relief efforts to the assumption of federal responsibility in the Federal Emergency Relief Program of 1933, to the transitional Civil Works Program in 1934, to a revised Federal Emergency Work Relief Program from mid-1934 through 1935, and finally to the Works Progress Administration (WPA) that dominated the scene from 1935 to 1940. Special programs for special groups of employables paralleled the above sequence: the National Youth Administration and the Civilian Conservation Corps provided work and income to youth, while the Public Works Administration stimulated employment by financing public construction projects.

The basic Federal Emergency Relief Program in 1933, a grant-in-aid program to the states, provided the initial bridge from state and local to federal responsibility for relieving depression destitution and unemployment. Under the Federal Emergency Relief Administration some 2 million persons were on emergency work programs in April and May of 1933. (For purposes of comparison, the population in 1933 was 125 million in contrast to 210 million in 1972.)

At the end of 1933 a short-term but highly important effort was made to combine recovery through enhanced purchasing power and relief in the Civil Works Program. In a short eight-month period almost one billion dollars was spent on projects to meet community needs, primarily roads and highways, repair and construction of public buildings, and various public services. At the program's peak, in January 1934, almost 4.3 million persons were at CWP work under specified prevailing wage and hour conditions.

Another short term and transitional program came between the Civil Works Program and WPA in 1935, the Emergency Work Relief Program. Essentially this joint federal-state effort continued the projects of CWP, but it limited wages earned and hours worked to what was needed to fill the "budgetary deficiency of the family." Earnings under this policy averaged about $5 per week. During the entire FERP and CWP period, work-relief and direct-relief were considerably mixed. Employables and unemployables were mixed in varying proportions as the adequacy of work-relief varied. The way was prepared

to abandon the grant-in-aid program of FERP and move to the federal
Works Progress Administration for employables and to the new 1935
Social Security Act public assistance program for the unemployable
needy.

The WPA—the Works Progress Administration retitled the Work
Projects Administration in July 1939—was established by executive
order of the President on May 6, 1935, under the authority of the
Emergency Relief Appropriation Act of 1935. It became and remains
the largest and most significant government direct-job-creation effort
ever undertaken in capitalist society.

The WPA provided that, under the terms set forth by the federal
government, local sponsors designed employment-creating projects.
After federal approval, federal funds were approved for each project
and a federal check was disbursed directly to each project worker.
Income for WPA workers was based on a ''security wage, which
ranged from $19 a month for unskilled Southern labor to $94 a month
for Northern urban professionals. When wages were raised by applying the prevailing wage rate principle, hours were reduced to preserve
the prescribed "security income" standard. Overall wages in 1940
were about $55 a month.

The significance of the WPA is multiple. About $10.5 billion
was spent on WPA projects from 1935 to 1940. Seventy-five percent
of this went into the wages of WPA workers, who reached a peak of
3.3 million in November 1938. The valuable results, and the concen-
trations of the projects are indicated by this summary of WPA work
between 1935 and 1940:

A. Construction: 79% of the total expenditures, with
         half new construction and half repairs.
         Highways and roads: 40% of all funds with
              565,000 miles of roads built or re-
              paired. Miles of curbs, drainage,
              guard rails and landscaping was pro-
              duced.
         Construction and repair of buildings: 28,000
              new buildings, 72,000 repaired or im-
              proved, additions to 3,600. Included
              are 4,800 new WPA school buildings,
              as well as libraries, hospitals, fire-
              houses, courthouses, etc.
         Flood and Erosion Control: jetties, break-
              waters, bulkheads, and riverbank and
              shore improvements.
         Recreation, Health, Sanitation: 2,750 athletic
              fields, 1,500 parks, 2,700 new

playgrounds and 9,000 repaired. 700
new swimming pools, 15,500 new recreational areas (tennis, handball, ski,
golf, outdoor theaters). Some 19,800
miles of new storm sewers and 12,700
miles of water mains.

National Defense and Aviation: Large number
of armed force buildings and extensive
airport facilities constructed.

B.   Public Service Projects (Non-Construction): White
collar projects took 21% of WPA funds and related especially to women, to technicians, professionals and clerical workers. The percentage
going into various activities suggests the applied
priorities: sewing, 6.6; research and surveys,
2.0; education, 2.0; recreation, 2.0; public re-
cords, 1.5; and library projects, 1.0. In one
month, October 1940, 245,000 men and women
were enrolled in WPA literacy and nationalization classes, and in the last three months of 1940,
WPA workers served 70 million lunches to children in 18,677 schools.[22]

From 1935 to 1940, the National Youth Administration provided
part-time work for about 400,000 ''in school'' youth each month, and
employment for some 300,000 out-of-school youth aged eighteen to
twenty-four each month. The Civilian Conservation Corps provided
work and some training to an average of 300,000 men each year from
1933 to 1941. Part of the physical accomplishments included planting
millions of trees and the building of 45,000 bridges, 6,800 dams, and
118,400 miles of truck trails and minor roads.

From the standpoint of current interests and issues, the experience of the 1930s with job creation suggests four major conclusions:

1. It is feasible for the government, through direct job creating
intervention, to create large-scale employment and to cut unemployment extensively.

2. The productive results of direct government job creation are
impressive and socially are dramatically useful.

3. The job programs of the 1930s were primitive by today's
standards. They did not include systematic or significant on-the-job
or off-the-job training, had no program of employability creating remedial or support services, and included nothing at all in the direction
of career development, upgrading, or upward mobility.

4. Expansion of the job creation programs was successfully
opposed by established political powers at all stages so that those

programs fell "far short of utilizing as fully as possible the idle economic resources at hand."[23]

The job creation activities of the New Deal did not approach the goal of high employment or of acceptable unemployment. That achievement was to require the spur provided by Hitler.

FULL EMPLOYMENT IN WORLD WAR II

As has already been noted, World War II led to an unprecedented and spectacular increase in the U.S. labor force, to the virtual extinction of unemployment, to full employment. The gross national product more than doubled from less than $100 billion in 1940 to $212 billion in 1945. Besides this growth some 12 million men and women were added to the armed services. Almost 8 million persons entered the labor force as a result of the aggregate demands of World War II, beyond the normally expected growth of the labor force due to population and secular change.

The major work force growth came from youth under twenty. Between April 1940 to April 1945 the labor force participation rate for boys was 57.1 percent instead of the projected 31.8 percent; for girls it was 33.9 percent instead of 16.8 percent. The second major source of labor was the adult female population: instead of an anticipated participation rate, for example, of 30.4 percent for women aged thirty-five to forty-four, the actual rate was 38.4 percent. A further sharp increase in labor force came from men over fifty-five. And as Durand notes, "Data on patients in mental institutions and on prisoners in state and federal penal institutions indicate that the institutional population grew more slowly during the war than would normally have been expected; if it did not actually decrease. A considerable contribution to the labor force probably came from this source."[24] There was a job for everyone.

The full employment of World War II resulted from three major factors:

1. Aggregate demand, in the Keynesian sense, grew as the gross national product (GNP) doubled and as the federal budget deficit averaged $50 billion ($250 billion in comparable 1972 GNP terms) for each of the years 1943, 1944, and 1945.

2. There was massive direct government "public service employment" created, both for 12 million in the armed forces and for millions more in the related supply services. National security expenditures equaled about 42 percent of GNP in 1943 and 1944.

3. Federal economic controls and planning took over the economy. The War Production Board planned output, allocated material and

production quotas, assigned priorities, and administered rationing of essential commodities. The office of Price Administration and the War Labor Board set prices, rents, and wages. In the labor supply area the War Manpower Commission, the Selective Service System, a federalized employment service and fair employment practices system controlled and guided—short of a general labor draft—the preparation, allocation, and utilization of all manpower.

It is easy but very unimaginative to ask, "If for war, why not for peace?" But the question does persist. And the conditions and procedures that led to our one clear experience with full employment remain as powerful and revealing guides for the future.

WORLD WAR II AND THE FULL EMPLOYMENT GOAL

The complex juxtaposition of the quick shift from depression to wartime full employment, the constructive and hopeful political and economic elan flowing from the defeat of the Axis in unity with the USSR, the possibly subtle challenge of the revolutionary and socialist alternatives—all combined to put full employment in the center of the contemplated postwar economic agenda. As Herbert Stein put it in an excellent discussion of this period:

> Full employment became the flag around which every one could rally. . . . Political leaders, government officials, and all private parties directly concerned with influencing economic policy came to give much higher priority to full employment in their own scale of national objectives for peacetime. They also came to believe that the "people" gave it such high priority that no political party or person could hope to be successful unless identified with the achievement of this goal. No party in office could remain in office without delivering full employment.[25]

But even as the rhetoric of full employment soared, political realities were at work to undermine and divert the integrity of the goal. As Stein remarks, there was uncertainty about "the degree of fullness," and the significant semantics began to mix the terms "high employment" and "full employment." The way began to be opened to supplant genuine full employment by spurious full employment so as to conform to the realities of economic-political power in the country.

Inextricably and perhaps fatally in the context of the growing opposition to planning, the full employment goal was seen as connected

with the concept of planning of the nation's economy. Throughout the
New Deal, the National Resources Planning Board (NRPB) created by
President Roosevelt in 1934 had studied, researched, and reported on
the theme of rational, planned use of all national resources. It reflected the mild "socialistic" inclinations of New Deal liberals such
as Rexford G. Tugwell, Mordecai Ezekiel, Leon Keyserling, and an
impressive group of liberal economists championing Keynesian economic intervention as essential to economic planning. In wartime this
agency was instructed to address the problem of conversion and the
postwar economy. Early in 1934 the NRPB submitted a lengthy program based on a "New Bill of Rights" and entitled Security, Work,
and Relief Policies. Submitted to Congress by President Roosevelt,
the first item in the "New Bill of Rights" was the "Right to work,
usefully and creatively through the productive years," and the second
item was "The right to fair pay, adequate to command the necessities
and amenities of life. . . . " The implications of this report were for
strong, central government planning and for drastic redistributive social and economic policies. Three months after the submission of this
report, Congress killed the National Resources Planning Board.[26]
This was a harbinger of the fact that, after lengthy and involved attention to the problems of postwar conversion, the aims of liberals for
"comprehensive planning for jobs" were to be effectively put aside
by the conservative force of Congress led by Senator George of
Georgia, who headed the Senate Finance Committee, and Republican
leaders such as Senator Robert Taft of Ohio. While the liberal-
conservative battle was to be resumed in the debate over the proposed
Full Employment Bill in 1945, the results were not to be changed.
The political-economic establishment as reflected in Congress was
not ready to commit the country to full employment or to authorize
the programs necessary for that objective, whether the issue rose
around postwar reconversion policy or legislation to guarantee jobs
for everyone.

    A wide range of authorities and political and economic leader-
ship had defined the full employment goal during World War II. In his
1944 annual address to Congress, Franklin D. Roosevelt formulated
a "Second Bill of Rights" with the first right being that of the "right
for all [to]. . . a useful and remunerative job in the industries or
shops or farms or mines of the nation. . . . " He asked Congress to
support government and planning agencies to provide the 60 million
jobs this goal required. On October 28, 1944, at Soldier's Field in
Chicago, while campaigning for reelection, the President restated the
goal of postwar full employment as "sixty million jobs." Henry A.
Wallace, then Vice President, put this into the title of his book, saying "I use the total of sixty million jobs as synonymous with the
peacetime requirements of full employment . . . work for everyone
who wants or needs it."[27]

Parallel to this liberal projection of full employment, business and conservative spokesmen began to endorse the aim of "full" or "high" employment, to be assured by government fiscal interventions if necessary. Thus, in 1942, Fortune magazine called upon government to guarantee full employment after the war.[28] The Republican candidate for President in 1944, Thomas Dewey, said in his nomination acceptance speech: "This must be a land where every man and woman has a fair chance to work and get ahead. Never again must free Americans face the specter of long-continued mass unemployment. We Republicans are agreed that full employment shall be a first objective of national policy. And by full employment, I mean a real chance for every man and woman to earn a decent living."[29]

Liberal businessmen in 1942 set up the Committee for Economic Development (CED), which aimed at "high employment" through Keynesian-type economic interventions. The limits of the CED insofar as full employment was concerned are suggested in the language employed by their then-leading spokesman, Beardsley Ruml of Macy's Department Store. Speaking in 1943, Ruml made reference to "high employment—as many jobs as we can—plenty of jobs—satisfactory high level of employment—the jobs we want."[30] This language represented more than simple semantic caution. Reflecting dominant enlightened business influence, it represented the diminution of the full employment goal that was really to control public policy after World War II. It certainly meant rejection of a return to Depression unemployment levels and a liberal acceptance of government Keynesian intervention for that objective. But it also meant that the establishment was not accepting a government commitment to guarantee any model of full employment. It was a "kiss of death."

Meanwhile, as World War II drew to a close, the issue of full employment claimed attention in important ways outside the United States. In great Britain, Sir William Beveridge prepared a highly influential report on full employment. Issued as a sequel to his earlier report on social insurance and allied services done for the British Government in 1942, Sir William's 1944 report assumed full employment as an essential government goal, commenting that "Acceptance of this new responsibility of the State, to be carried out by whatever Government may be in power, marks the line which we must cross, in order to pass from the old Britain of mass unemployment and jealousy and fear to the new Britain of opportunity and service to all."[31] As already noted, Sir William meant that everything except short-term frictional unemployment should be eliminated. In the context of a postwar orientation to the new welfare state in Great Britain, Beveridge's emphasis had great significance.

Of even greater significance was the United Nations Charter, drafted at San Francisco. It contained a clear commitment to full employment. Article 55 of the charter states:

With a view of the creation of conditions of stability and well being which are necessary for peaceful and friendly relations among nations based on respect for the principle of equal rights and self determination of peoples, the United Nations shall promote:
  a. higher standards of living, full employment, and conditions of economic and social progress and development.

And Article 56 sets forth the obligation that

All members pledge themselves to take joint and separate action in cooperation with the Organization for the achievement of the purposes set forth in Article 55.

Subsequently, on December 10, 1948, the United Nations Assembly at Paris adopted "The Universal Declaration of Human Rights," which stated as a "common standard of achievement for all peoples and nations" the proposition in Article 23 that:

1. Everyone has the right to work, to free choice of employment, to just and favorable conditions of work and to protection against unemployment.
2. Everyone, without any discrimination, has the right to equal pay for equal work.
3. Everyone who works has the right to just and favorable remuneration, insuring for himself and his family an existence worthy of human dignity. . . .

Then again on November 25, 1949, in Resolution 308 (IV), the UN General Assembly restated the full employment pledge as involving agreement to "take action, as the need arises, designed to promote and maintain full and productive employment, through measures appropriate to its political, economic and social institutions."

"A Group of Experts"—five distinguished economists from Western capitalist countries—appointed by the UN secretary-general to report on national and international measures for full employment in 1949, properly described these United Nation's actions, holding that

The full employment pledge embodied in the United Nations Charter marks a historic phase in the evolution of the modern conception of the functions and responsibilities of the democratic State. With other international agreements and declarations of national policy by

individual countries it reflects the fundamental importance
of the promotion of full employment from two distinct
points of view: first, as a condition of economic and social
progress and an essential factor in human rights—a goal
adopted by each State in the interests of its own citizens,
irrespective of any international repercussions; and, sec-
ondly, as a necessary prerequisite for the maintenance and
smooth working of an international economic system and
"the achievement of a stable and expanding world economy."[32]

These UN actions surrounded in time the debate in the U.S. Congress on proposed full employment legislation. The reactions of the
U.S. Government to the UN policy developments is therefore of special
interest and significance. A bitter battle was waged in San Francisco
by Senators Arthur Vandenberg (R-Michigan) and Thomas Connally
(D-Texas) against the use of the term "full employment." As the major foreign affairs leaders in the U.S. Senate and as leaders of the
U.S. delegation to the San Francisco UN Conference, Vandenberg and
Connally threatened Senate rejection of the charter if the "full employment" phrase was used, and they ordered Barnard College dean
Virginia Gildersleeve, as a U.S. member of the drafting committee,
to seek to substitute the phrase "high and stable levels of employment." By face saving maneuvers, the U.S. delegation finally accepted
the "full employment" words insisted upon by the majority of the
drafting committee.[33]

A similar conflict occurred in August 1949 when the UN Economic and Social Council (ECOSOC) debated the question of unemployment.
Conflicting resolutions were considered. One representing the Commu-
nist UN members was submitted by the World Federation of Trade
Unions and sponsored by Poland; the other was proposed by the dele-
gates of France, the United States, and Great Britain. The WFTU-
Poland resolution was defeated and the joint American-British-French
resolution was approved. For our immediate purpose, a difference
that developed on the joint resolution is of significance. In the original
version, reference was to a "high level of employment" rather than to
the UN Charter expression "full employment." The Australian delegate proposed an amendment to restore the "full employment" phrase.
The U.S. delegate, named Stinebower, defended the "high employment"
phrase and asked the Australian to withdraw his amendment. Supported by the British delegate, the Australian insisted on "full employment" and the phrase was restored.[34]

It was at this period that the "Group of Experts" was appointed
by the UN secretary general to report on actions taken and required
to carry out the UN full employment mandate. The report, unanimously

agreed to by five distinguished Western economists, was described by one observer:

> The report runs counter to the whole stand taken by dele-
> gates trying to water down the full employment obligation.
> It defines full employment, it makes its maintenance a
> "must," it calls for governmental controls and plans in
> domestic economy and subordination of national foreign
> trade and investment policy to inter-governmental and
> expert decisions. An unsung burial of this unpleasing
> document would seem to be indicated.[35]

This prophecy made in 1951 would seem, in 1972, to have been essentially accurate.

THE FULL EMPLOYMENT BILL VERSUS
THE EMPLOYMENT ACT—1945-46

In 1945 and 1946 Congress defeated the Murray-Wagner[36] Full Employment Bill and enacted the Whittington-Taft Employment Act of 1946. The significance of this action is almost universally unrecognized. Indeed there is a widespread illusion that, instead of refusing to pass a full employment act, Congress actually did so. Thus for example, the final report of the National Commission on the Causes and Prevention of Violence in 1969 referred with great favor in its introduction to the actions flowing from the "Full Employment Act of 1946."[37] And on television in 1972, CBS commentator Eric Sevareid extolled the virtue of the "Full Employment Act" as an indicator of national economic responsibility.

The defeat of the Full Employment Bill was a strong and purposeful affirmative action against a national commitment to full employment, and against the idea of government action either by fiscal spending actions or job creation to guarantee jobs for all. It represented a defeat for the whole body of thought and political influence that had pursued the idea of strong government intervention, planning, and economic action to eliminate unemployment. The passage of the employment act vaguely reflected the acceptance of government responsibility to avoid massive unemployment, but it provided neither clear commitment nor the means to maintain any defined level of high employment. It sanctified the acceptance of "spurious full employment" as our national obligation.

The account of this legislative event has been extensively and expertly reported, most notably in Stephen Kemp Bailey's Congress

<u>Makes a Law</u>; it need not be repeated here.[38] The essential elements
of the issue are clear. The Murray-Wagner bill stated the objective
to be "a national policy and program for assuring continuing full employment" and stated the meaning of this objective to be that "All
Americans able to work and seeking work have the right to useful,
remunerative, regular, and full-time employment, and it is the policy
of the United States to assure the existence at all times of sufficient
employment opportunities to enable all Americans who have finished
their schooling and who do not have full-time housekeeping responsibilities freely to exercise this right."

To realize the goal of full employment the President was directed to furnish Congress each year with a "National Production
and Employment Budget," which would include a program for whatever federal investment and spending was necessary "to assure continuing full employment."

The counterproposal that became the Employment Act of 1946,
after changing "full" to "high" in the House of Representatives,
settled for a final version using the phrase "maximum employment,
production, and purchasing power." This objective was to be pursued
"in a manner calculated to foster and promote free competitive enterprise" and set up the Council of Economic Advisors and the Congressional Joint Economic Committee to submit reports and recommend
actions and legislation to achieve the stated objective.

The confrontation posed the liberal-labor bloc against the conservative, business, and southern bloc both inside and outside Congress. The result was neither an impasse nor a compromise; it was
a clear-cut victory for the conservative bloc. It is true that while
Senator Murray expressed "great disappointment" in the act, he
urged its final support saying that "it contained all the essentials of
a full employment program."[39] Some forty labor and liberal groups
who had supported the original full employment bill, likewise expressed disappointment while urging President Truman to approve
the measure. Indicating hope for good results if the act were "adequately implemented," this group, however, prophetically concluded:
"Unless, however, the act is adequately implemented, history will
record it as a mockery and an affront to the millions of Americans
who are determined that our free institutions shall not again be threatened by the curse of unemployment."[40] The President responded with
a hopeful and supportive approval of the Employment Act of 1946.

Senator Robert Taft (R-Ohio), who had led the fight against the
Full Employment bill, was far more accurate when, in the final debate, he told the Senate, "I do not think any Republican need fear vot-
ing for the bill because of any apprehension that there is a victory in
the passage of the full employment bill, because there is no full employment bill anymore."[41]

NOTES

1. William H. Beveridge, Full Employment In a Free Society (New York: W. W. Norton, 1945), pp. 18-20.

2. National and International Measures For Full Employment, United Nations, E/1584 22 December 1949, pp. 11-15. The members of the Group of Experts appointed by Secretary General Trygve Lie in pursuance of a Resolution of the Economic and Social Council were John Maurice Clark, Professor of Economics at Columbia University; Arthur Smithies, Professor of Economics at Harvard University; Nicholas Kaldor, Fellow of Kings College, Cambridge; Pierre Uri, Economic and Financial Advisor to the Commissariat general du Plan, Paris; and E. Ronald Walker, Economic Advisor to the Australian Department of External Affairs.

3. John D. Durand, The Labor Force in the United States 1890-1960 (New York: Social Service Research Council, 1948), pp. 137-60. Clarence D. Long, The Labor Force in War and Transition: Four Countries (New York: National Bureau of Economic Research, 1952), p. 1.

4. Murray Feshbach, "Manpower Trends in the USSR: 1950 to 1980" (Mimeographed, Washington, D.C.: Bureau of the Census, U.S. Department of Commerce, May 1971), p. 1.

5. National and International Measures, pp. 6-7.

6. Joseph A. Schumpeter, History of Economic Analysis (New York: Oxford University Press, 1954), pp. 270-72.

7. Michael Harrington, "Government Should Be the Employer of First Resort," The New York Times Magazine, March 26, 1972, p. 44.

8. Edward Bellamy, Looking Backward—2000-1887 (New York: Houghton Mifflin Co., 1887), p. 62.

9. Alfred Marshall, Principles of Economics (London: Macmillan, 1930).

10. H. Stanley Jevons, The Causes of Unemployment (London: Alabaster, Passmore and Sons, 1909).

11. Schumpeter, op. cit., p. 1135.

12. David Weintraub, "Unemployment and Increasing Productivity," in Technological Trends and National Policy, National Resources Committee, June 1937, 75th Congress, 1st session, House Document No. 360 (Washington, D.C., 1937), p. 70.

13. John Maynard Keynes, The General Theory of Employment, Interest, and Money (New York: Harcourt, Brace and Company, 1936). Among the enormous literature relating to The General Theory, two volumes are of special general interest: Robert Lekachman, The Age of Keynes (New York: Random House, 1966); and Herbert Stein, The Fiscal Revolution in America (Chicago: University of Chicago Press, 1969).

14. Byrd L. Jones, "The Role of Keynesians in Wartime Policy and Postwar Planning, 1940-46," American Economic Review, LXII, 2 (May 1972), 125-33.

15. The title of a recent article in the Brookings Papers on Economic Activity by Robert E. Hall "Why is the Unemployment Rate So High at Full Employment?," expresses the contradiction.

16. Richard Gilbert, et al., An Economic Program for American Democracy (New York: Vanguard, 1938), p. 80.

17. Mordecai Ezekiel, Jobs For All: Through Industrial Expansion (New York: Alfred A. Knopf, 1939), pp. xii, 7.

18. National Resources Committee, The Structure of the American Economy: Part I. Basic Characteristics (Washington, D.C., June 1939), pp. 2, 371.

19. Bernard M. Baruch, American Industry in the War, A Report of the War Industries Board (March 1921) (New York: Prentice-Hall, 1941).

20. Ibid., p. 96.

21. Arthur E. Burns and Edward A. Williams, Federal Work, Security, and Relief Programs, WPA Research Monograph XXIV, 1941; reprinted by De Capo Press, New York, 1971, p. 74. Material in this section is based on this excellent and authoritative monograph prepared in the Division of Research, Works Progress Administration.

22. Burns and Williams, op. cit., pp. 58-60.

23. Ibid., p. 75.

24. Durand, op. cit., pp. 145-46.

25. Stein, op. cit., pp. 170-75.

26. Stephen K. Bailey, Congress Makes A Law: The Story Behind the Employment Act of 1946 (New York: Columbia University Press, 1950). Every writer in this area relies, as I have, on this authoritative account. See especially pp. 13-36.

27. Henry A. Wallace, Sixty Million Jobs (New York: Reynal and Hitchcock, Simon and Schuster, 1945), p. 3.

28. Fortune, December 1942.

29. The New York Times, June 29, 1944; quoted in Stein, op. cit., p. 173.

30. Beardsley Ruml, "Financing Post-War Prosperity—Controlling Booms and Depressions," delivered over NBC radio network, and reprinted in Vital Speeches, November 15, 1943, pp. 95-96. Quoted in Stein, op. cit., pp. 185-6.

31. Beveridge, op. cit., p. 29.

32. National and International Measures For Full Employment, op. cit., p. 5.

33. Based on Bailey, op. cit., pp. 102-03, who reports a newspaper account by Drew Pearson in "Washington Merry-Go-Round,"

The Washington Post, June 3, 1945. This whole episode needs further clarification and research.

34. John Maclaurin, The United Nations and Power Politics (London: Allen and Unwin, 1951), pp. 272-90.

35. Maclaurin, op. cit., pp. 289-90.

36. Democratic Senators Thomas (Utah), O'Mahoney (Wyoming), and Republican Senators Morse (Oregon), Tobey (New Hampshire), Aiken (Vermont) and Langer (North Dakota) also sponsored the bill, S380.

37. National Commission on the Causes and Prevention of Violence, To Establish Justice, To Insure Domestic Tranquility (Washington, D.C., December 1969), p. xxx.

38. See in other sources already cited: Lekachman, op. cit., pp. 165-75; Stein, op. cit., pp. 197-204; also Leon Keyserling, "Keynesian Revolution-Discussion," American Economic Review, May 1972, pp. 135-36; and Edwin G. Nourse, Economics in the Public Service (New York: Harcourt, Brace and Company, 1953), pp. 335-67.

39. Congressional Record, February 8, 1946.

40. Nourse, op. cit., pp. 339-40.

41. Congressional Record, February 8, 1946.

CHAPTER

2

FULL EMPLOYMENT IN THE NEW "DAY OF THE DINOSAUR"

Bertram M. Gross

The proposed "Equal Opportunity and Full Employment Act of 1976," otherwise known as the Hawkins-Humphrey Job Guarantee Bill, is a measure that is at once overdue, timely, and ahead of its time. First, it proposes to help make a reality of the "unalienable rights" declared by the Founding Fathers almost 200 years ago, of the Economic Bill of Rights transmitted to Congress by President Roosevelt in 1944, and of the hopes raised by the passage of the Employment Act in 1946. Second, the congressional hearings on the new legislation were opened before the House Subcommittee on Equal Opportunities in October 1974, when for the first time in its history America was experiencing rampant inflation, a collapsing stock market, and the beginnings of a recession, all together. The sponsors of the measure see in it a democratic and constitutional path out of this unprecedented crisis which has struck not only America but all the other "advanced" capitalist countries. Third, the measure is ahead of its time in that congressional action has begun at a time when the dead hand of the past still wields a baneful influence in business circles, the White House, the Congress, and the universities. The high priests of Nixonomics still cater to the most backward leanings of banking and corporate elites. The Keynesians are still fighting old wars with the scribblings of a somewhat defunct economist while looking fondly in the rear-view mirror to admire their self-styled "fine tuning" of fiscal affairs during the Vietnam war. And a grisly array of doddering dinosaurs are calling for more unemployment and reduced social services in order to slow down the inflation.

Originally published in Social Policy 5, no. 5 (January/February 1975), pp. 20-33. © 1975 by Social Policy Corporation.

To provide any deep perspective on the proposed legislation, it would be necessary to compare today's strange new world with that simple old world of 1944. It would be necessary to review the immense changes in technology, corporate organization, foreign economic and political relations, public bureaucracies, and America's "subwelfare state." It would be imperative to review both the "revolution of rising expectations" on the part of previously submerged groups and the slowly rising wave of "benign authoritarianism" (or "friendly fascism") and other tendencies toward a new corporate society. All these matters necessarily enter into any serious discussion of planning for genuine full employment without inflation.

My present, more modest intentions will be confined to (1) a 30-year retrospect on full employment legislation, (2) a brief summary of the major shifts in legislative content, from the original Full Employment Bill to the Employment Act of 1946 to the proposed 1976 act, and (3) some comments on the relation between genuine full employment and modern capitalism in both its American and multinational forms.

"FULL" AND "MAXIMUM" EMPLOYMENT: ROOSEVELT TO NIXON

Thirty years ago, while war was raging in Europe and Asia, we had genuine full employment in America. Everyone able and willing to work had a range of choices—even women, older people, youngsters, and Black people. Some, of course, had more choices than others. But almost anyone could walk out of one job and find another. To keep people on their payrolls, employers had to provide better wages, better working conditions, more challenging work, and, in some cases, a little participation in management. The only people without job choices were the 16.4 million men and women in the armed forces.

But none of us who were members of the depression generation thought that full employment could survive the war. We feared a return to bread lines, riots at factory gates, apple sellers on street corners, veterans killed in bonus marches, banks closing down, and bankers jumping out of windows.

Running for his fourth term in office, Franklin Roosevelt responded to this fear by promising jobs for all after the war—60 million civilian jobs. Candidate Thomas Dewey promised the same and so did most Democratic and Republican candidates for Congress and state and local office. But some strong-willed members of Congress were not impressed by these vague promises. They wanted a specific and comprehensive legislative program. Also, they were sick

and tired of being transmission belts for proposals from the White
House. They drafted many of their own bills.

At that time I was fully employed night and day by a Senate
subcommittee[1] headed by two of those strong-willed members:
James E. Murray of Montana and Harry S. Truman of Missouri. On
their behalf I had also been working closely for many years with
Rep. Wright Patman of Texas, then chairman of the House Committee
on Small Business. A few days after Roosevelt and Truman won the
1944 election, I was asked to prepare a subcommittee report on "Legislation for Reconversion and Full Employment." This report, made
public on December 18, 1944, declared that "unless an economic substitute is found for war contracts, mass unemployment will become
a serious threat and the number of unemployed men and women in this
country could easily surpass anything that was dreamed of during the
last depression."

Senators Murray and Truman (who was also vice-president-
elect) pointed out that "as yet, unfortunately, we do not have an 'adequate program' to provide 60 million productive jobs." They went on
to state that "the so-called right to a job is a meaningless figure of
speech unless our Government assumes responsibility for the expansion of our economy so that it will be capable of assuring full employment." They then presented, for preliminary discussion before introduction, the first draft of "The Full Employment Act of 1945."

The Truman Compromise of 1946

The Murray-Truman proposal stirred up huge waves of newspaper comment and congressional interest. Indeed, the 14 months from
December 1944 to February 1946, when Truman, as president, signed
the Employment Act, covered a period of great turmoil and confusion
which is described in Stephen Bailey's prize-winning book Congress
Makes a Law (Columbia University Press, 1950). A tangled web of
debate swirled through the Congress, executive agencies, and across
the country. What was really meant by "full employment"? people
asked. Could or should the "right to a job" be guaranteed? How far
should the federal government go in maintaining prosperity? What
kind of agency should try to coordinate the federal hodge-podge of
government economic programs? And more specifically, what should
be the content of 100 or so different programs and policies affecting
the level of employment and output and the nature of economic relations with other countries?

Conflicting views on all these matters were expressed in divergent amendments to the original Full Employment Bill. These con-

flicts were reconciled in an historic compromise. On the one hand, the
Congress rejected the right to employment opportunities promised by
Roosevelt; on the other hand, the essence of the 1946 legislation was
its expression of a new commitment by the federal government never
again to allow another mass depression. While this compromise dis-
tressed many of the bill's most ardent supporters, there is no doubt
that the Employment Act of 1946 represented an historic turning point
in American history. Thus, an eminent George Washington University
law professor has declared that the Employment Act of 1946, "although
a statute, in its importance may be said to have made constitutional
law."[2]

Executive Amendments

        Since 1946, official amendments to the Employment Act have
dealt with technical details only: the date of the President's Economic
Report, the structure of the Council of Economic Advisers, the name
and structure of the Joint Economic Committee, and the limitations
on council and committee appropriations. Legislative action has never
been taken on various proposals to include "price stability" on a par
with "maximum employment, production and purchasing power" in the
act's declaration of policy.
        But in a more meaningful sense the Employment Act of 1946 has
been continuously amended by administrative fiat. Six presidents—
Truman, Eisenhower, Kennedy, Johnson, Nixon and now Ford—have
given it widely different interpretations. These in turn have been the
outcome of fundamental changes in the dynamics of American capitalism and in the conflicting concepts and values of different groups in
American society in a period of rapid and confusing change throughout
the world. Specifically, three "real-life amendments" have been
arrived at through changing interpretations of the Employment Act of
1946: (1) the shift from countercyclical stabilization to sustained economic growthmanship; (2) the expansion of growthmanship to include
the quality of life as well as the quantity of goods and services; and
(3) the interpretation of "maximum employment" as a rising level of
politically tolerable unemployment.
        When the Employment Act was first passed, it was generally
regarded as a countercyclical measure whose main purpose was to
see that the government reacted positively to any threat of depression.
But under President Truman the emphasis shifted from antidepres-
sion stabilization to the prevention of depression by sustained economic growth. Thus the Truman council always emphasized "stable

growth'' instead of plain old stability. For a while the GNP growthmanship initiated under Leon H. Keyserling's leadership of the Truman
council was viewed askance by conservatives. But eventually it was
picked up by the Rockefeller Brothers Fund in the late 1950s, used by
Nixon in his 1960 campaign, and then made into almost a household
word by the council under Kennedy.[3]

Under Johnson the ante was raised still higher. In May 1964, in
preparation for his re-election to the presidency, Johnson called for
a Great Society that ''rests on abundance and liberty for all'' and ''demands an end to poverty and racial injustice, to which we are totally
committed in our time.'' For the next few years, despite the agonies
of the expanding Vietnam war, the Johnson administration's economic
program was oriented toward ''quality of life'' objectives with stable
growth.

A third process of executive amendment, initiated during the
Eisenhower years—the acceptance of increasingly higher levels of
officially reported unemployment—represented a clear willingness to
use unemployment as a means of keeping prices down. The result
was not merely a generally higher official unemployment situation
than under Truman but also a specific unemployment situation that
helped defeat Republican candidates in the 1960 election. Under
Richard Nixon the policy of tolerating increased unemployment not
only returned but was converted into an open policy of promoting increased unemployment as a presumed anti-inflation measure. Apart
from the period immediately preceding his re-election in 1972, when
brakes were taken off and economic expansion was accelerated, this
policy has been adhered to since. Even today when America is suffering the most devastating inflation in peacetime history, the Employment Act of 1946 is interpreted by Nixon's appointee in the White
House as authorizing a president's economic program that tolerates
rising unemployment.

In part, the ''Equal Opportunity and Full Employment Act of
1976'' is a reaction to this unwarranted interpretation. But it is much
more than that. It represents the first effort to amend and extend the
1946 law by decisions openly arrived at in Congress rather than by
the fiat of a quasi-imperial presidency. It is also an effort to provide
for the kind of balanced economic growth that will prevent future depressions and take us out of the present recession without undue pressures on either the level of prices or the supply of energy and raw
material resources. Above all, it aims at achieving the high goals of
ending poverty and racial injustice by the simplest, most direct, and
most effective of all possible methods: namely, providing that every
adult American able and willing to work—regardless of sex, age, race,
color, religion, or national origin—has the guaranteed right to opportunities for useful employment at fair rates of compensation.

SHIFTS IN LEGISLATIVE CONTENT:
1944, 1946, 1976

Let us now concentrate on the major changes in strictly legislative policy as the original Full Employment Bill was converted into
the Employment Act of 1946 and as the 1946 statute would be extended
by enactment of the new proposal. I shall not attempt at this time the
ultra-precise comparisons that should eventually be made available
to the Congress and the public but concentrate instead on ten broad
shifts of strategic rather than tactical or technical significance.

Personal Rights

All the earlier versions of the Full Employment Bill contained
some version of Roosevelt's "right to a useful and remunerative job
in the industries, or shops, or farms or mines of the Nation." The
version reported favorably to the floor of the Senate on September 22,
1945 read as follows: "All Americans able to work and desiring to
work are entitled to an opportunity to useful, remunerative, regular
and full-time employment " (Section 2-b), and went on to declare that
"the Federal government has the responsibility to assure continuing
full employment, that is, the existence at all times of sufficient employment opportunities for all Americans able to work and desiring to
work" (Section 2-c). The legislative record makes it clear, however,
that this was not regarded as an individual right. Nor were there
either administrative or judicial procedures through which an appeal
could be launched by people whose rights were denied.

In the Employment Act of 1946 no mention was made of either
rights or entitlement. Similarly, the ideal of assuring or guaranteeing
a full employment level of production was also dropped.

In going back to the older idea of human rights, the new legislation clarifies a number of points:

1. The right set forth in the bill is an individual right.
2. It is a right to opportunities.
3. It is a right not just for any sort of opportunities but
   rather to opportunities "for useful paid employment
   at fair rates of compensation."
4. It is the responsibility of the federal government to
   enforce this right.
5. Any person who believes his/her right has been vio-
   lated has access to both administrative and judicial
   appeal procedures.

Equal Opportunity

The earliest versions of the Full Employment Bill presumably conferred job rights on "all" Americans. Unfortunately, the authors of the bill were not then sufficiently aware that unless the word "all" is clearly spelled out, it has always tended to mean "all, but." (Even the Declaration of Independence stated that "all men" are created equal, and it is not clear whether or not the Founding Fathers included the Founding Mothers.) The ambiguity in the bill was resolved in the wrong direction by the January 1945 version, which specifically limited the assurance of employment opportunities to "all Americans who have finished their schooling and who do not have full-time housekeeping responsibilities."

While the Employment Act of 1946 does not contain this exclusion, it does not use the word "all." And during the 29 years since its enactment, it has become abundantly clear that except for the right to sit in restaurants and ride in the front seats of buses, all Americans have not had equal opportunities in such fundamental areas as jobs, housing, and education.

The new Hawkins-Humphrey bill defines "all" as "really all with no fine print exceptions or reservations." It guarantees the employment rights of <u>every</u> adult American regardless of "sex, age, race, color, religion or national origin." It also specifically provides for special counseling, training, or other assistance for "such individuals and groups as may face special obstacles in finding and holding useful and rewarding employment." This provision refers to the following specific categories:

1. those suffering from past or present discrimination or bias on the basis of sex, age, race, color, religion or national origin,
2. older workers and retirees,
3. the physically or mentally handicapped,
4. youths to age 21,
5. potentially employable recipients of public assistance,
6. the inhabitants of depressed areas, urban and rural,
7. veterans of the armed forces,
8. people unemployed because of the relocation, closing, or reduced operations in industrial or military facilities, and
9. such other groups as the president or the Congress may designate from time to time.

Full Employment

None of the earliest versions of the Full Employment Bill had
a clear-cut concept of full employment. The December 1944 version
contained an involved definition that picked up some of the worst elements in the depression-era concept of "labor force" as limited to
those working plus those actively seeking work. This limitation was
continued in the January 1945 version, which limited the "right" to
those "able to work and seeking work" and (as already indicated) further restricted the government's responsibility to "those Americans
who have finished their schooling and who do not have full-time housekeeping responsibilities." In the bill reported to the Senate these re-
strictions were dropped and the term "full employment" was preceded
by the word "continuing."

In the Employment Act, the term "full" was dropped completely.
In its place, the declaration of policy committed the federal government to promoting "maximum employment, production and purchasing
power." By itself, the word "maximum" is at least as strong as, if
not stronger than, "full." In context, however, the sum total of changes
left the level of desired employment rather loose and open to the en-
suing interpretations of a steadily rising level of officially defined unemployment and officially ignored hidden unemployment.

The Hawkins-Humphrey proposal not only goes back to "full
employment;" it provides the first clear-cut legislative definition:
" 'Full Employment' is a situation under which there are useful and
rewarding employment opportunities for all adult Americans able and
willing to work." (Section 11-2). Moreover, it clearly mandates the
broadening of the present labor force concept (which was adopted during the depression period as a way of minimizing the reported size
of the labor supply) to all the labor potentialities represented by those
adults able and willing to work. Thus the annual Labor Reports of the
President would account for

the changing volume and composition of the American
labor supply, by major areas of the country, with special
emphasis on the total number of people able and willing
to work under varying conditions of remuneration and
suitability, the extent of various forms of involuntary unemployment (including those not working or seeking to
work but able and willing to work if suitable opportunities
were presented, and those between jobs), estimates of
recent, present and prospective shortfalls in private and
public employment opportunities, the impact of mobility

and immigration, and the volume of national product lost
by such waste or insufficient use of available labor power.
(Section 3-b)

Above all, there is clear recognition of the need for a larger
proportion of part-time job opportunities and the possibilities inherent
in an expansion of voluntary leisure.

President's Program

The first versions of the Full Employment Bill provided for a
macroeconomic analysis and program called the National Production
and Employment Budget. In the Employment Act this was renamed
the Economic Report of the President. Its macroeconomic nature was
unchanged, but there was less commitment to attaining the "needed
levels" of employment, production, and purchasing power.

In the new legislation, the president is responsible for formu-
lating a two-part full employment program which assures macroeconomic planning grounded in a wide variety of specific policies and
programs. The first part of the program, contained in the President's
Economic Report, provides a macroeconomic approach to the levels
of employment, production, and expenditures required to meet "human and national needs." But it is also disaggregated by sectors and
program areas. The second part, in the President's annual Labor Reports (previously called Manpower Reports), deals with the characteristics of the labor supply and the varying needs and potentialities of
people able and willing to work.

Executive Agencies

In the first versions of the Full Employment Bill the burden of
integration and coordination of the many executive agencies whose
policies and programs bear on the level of employment and output was
placed squarely on the president. The final Employment Act provided
for the Council of Economic Advisers as a staff arm of the president.
The new legislation goes one step further by assigning major functions
to the Department of Labor and the U.S. Full Employment Service as
participants in planning and administering employment policy.

Local Participation

While the first versions of the Full Employment Bill and the statute itself referred to some vaguely defined form of consultation with state and local governments, the new proposal goes much further. Building on the Comprehensive Employment and Training Act of 1973, it confers major planning functions on the local councils set up by local governments (the "prime sponsors" under the CETA legislation). It also adds a provision for community or neighborhood boards.

Joint Congressional Committee

The first proposals provided for a Joint Congressional Committee which, in addition to reviewing the president's proposed economic program, would also present to both houses of the Congress a joint resolution setting forth guides to budgetary policy. The joint resolution provision was dropped on the floor of the Senate and never restored.

The new legislation proposes to restore this form of legislative initiative on the part of the Joint Economic Committee. It states this function in a form that is appropriately tied in with the work of the Appropriations Committees and the newly established Joint Budget Committee. The new legislation also mandates extensive local hearings by the appropriate committees of the Congress on all relevant aspects of the act's administration.

Appeals Machinery

Neither the early versions of the Full Employment Bill nor the 1946 statute contained any appeal machinery. In contrast, the new proposal is very clear on this point. Section 5-g provides for administrative appeal procedures to be set up by the Secretary of Labor. Section 5-h provides for "injunctive, declaratory and other forms of relief, including damages" through appeals to the U.S. district courts.

Full Employment Research

Although neither the original proposals nor the 1946 statute mentioned research specifically, the need for some types of research was indirectly implied at all stages.

The new proposal, in contrast, sets up a new National Commission for Full Employment Policy Studies (Section 9). A specific, although not exclusive, mandate is provided for a dozen specific areas of research on full employment policy. The first of these areas, for example, is "the policies and programs needed to reduce whatever inflationary pressures may result from full employment, to manage any such inflationary pressures through appropriate fiscal policies and indirect and direct controls, and to protect the weaker groups in society from whatever inflationary trends cannot be avoided or controlled." And to emphasize the many noneconomic aspects of genuine full employment policies, research is also to be done on "a comprehensive program for such economic and social indicators, both quantitative and qualitative, as may be needed for the continuous and objective monitoring of basic economic and social trends in the performance, structure and environment of the American economy and society." Above all, divergent approaches will be encouraged to each area of policy study.

Private Business

The first versions of the original Full Employment Bill in 1944 and 1945 gave the highest priority to private investment and expanded activity in the private sector. In the 1946 statute, with the role of federal expenditures relatively reduced, still higher priority was given to federal activity to promote the expansion of private business. This was stated in terms of the federal government's responsibility to maintain employment opportunities "in a manner calculated to foster and promote free competitive enterprise and the general welfare." Although this priority was often interpreted as referring to all private enterprises, including the huge oligopolies in administered price sectors of imperfect competition, the legislative record shows an intention to foster and promote business competition, not oligopoly.

The new legislation, in contrast, escapes this ambiguity by avoiding any distinctive priority. Both private and public employment trends and needs are included in the President's Full Employment and Production Program (Section 3). Both are included in the reservoirs of public and private employment to be developed under the local governments' local planning councils (Section 4). The Job Guarantee Office of the U.S. Full Employment Service may draw on such reservoirs by entering "into agreements with public agencies and private organizations operating on a profit, non-profit or limited-profit basis" (Section 5).

JOB RIGHTS UNDER CAPITALISM

Can genuine and continuing full employment be assured under modern Capitalism?

Conventional economic theorists such as Milton Friedman, Paul Samuelson, and John K. Galbraith artfully dodge this question by relying on superficial concepts of full employment, ridiculous models of modern capitalism, or both.

Socialist economists have done a little better in looking at both unemployment and capitalism. They were not only the first to regard depression as a subject worthy of attention by economists; they were also the first to bring the concept of capitalism into use. And most Marxians do have an answer to the question—a negative one. According to Marx, the "reserve army of the unemployed is the lever of capitalist accumulation." It helps the capitalists keep wages down to exploitative levels, thereby building up surplus value. This reserve army can be put to work only through armament booms, wars, imperialist expansion, or slave labor under police or military control. Today's Marxians generally maintain that sustained and genuine full employment without war, imperialism, or inflation is possible only under some form of "socialism," whatever that means. If one suggests that something very close to genuine full employment has been sustained for many years in the capitalist societies of West Germany, Sweden, Japan, and Israel, their answer is apt to be, "Just you wait . . . That may all be ended by the impending world monetary crisis and the recession that is deepening in the United States."

In this paper I shall resist the temptation to go further into either theoretical debates or the full employment achievements in other capitalist countries. Rather, I shall concentrate on the more antediluvian positions and policies of American business both 30 years ago and today.

THE OLD ATTACK ON FULL EMPLOYMENT

When the original Full Employment Bill was first proposed in 1944 and introduced in 1945, it found some supporters among small and independent business, some business leaders involved in government affairs (such as Edward Stettinius, former head of U.S. Steel), and—with some modifications—among many of the business executives associated with the National Planning Association and the newly established Committee for Economic Development. This showing of friendliness or studied neutrality misled many economists (particularly those whose economic models excluded all information on conflicts of economic interest) into naive assertions that <u>everyone</u> was for full employment.

But as soon as legislation was introduced to bring full employment discussions down to reality, a frenetic outcry against the bill was raised by the organized dinosaurs of the big business community—mainly, the National Association of Manufacturers, the U.S. Chamber of Commerce, and the so-called Committee for Constitutional Government. As Stephen Bailey revealed in <u>Congress Makes a Law,</u> there was concrete agitation and propaganda in almost every congressional district in the country.

In reporting the amended Full Employment Bill to the Senate, the majority of the Senate Banking and Currency Committee summarized the three major arguments made by the opponents of full employment.[4] The first argument was that continuing full employment is impossible under our "free enterprise economic system." Thus William L. Kleitz, vice-president of the Guaranty Trust Company, testified that depressions "are inevitable under the free enterprise system and that the best we can do is to limit their depth and their durations." This argument was enlarged on by another business witness who suggested that "we will always have these [depressions] because that is human nature . . . it cannot be overturned by laws and it cannot be changed by laws." It was carried still further by the Citizens National Committee, Inc., which called the full employment objective "dubious" and suggested it could be obtained only "during relatively brief periods of extraordinary wartime activity" or else by "adoption of a totalitarian form of economy." The New York State Chamber of Commerce circulated a bulletin in March 1945 stating that depressions are "the price we pay for freedom."

The majority of the Senate Banking Committee responded to this argument by maintaining that "continuing full employment is possible under our economic system. We believe that full employment and free enterprise are entirely compatible." The committee majority then went on to make the following counterattack: "Those who argue that continuing full employment means regimentation are themselves sowing the seeds of economic and political revolution. No hostile foreign agent could do more to wreck the fabric of our society than to tell our people that unemployment is the price we pay for free enterprise . . ." The committee report also reminded the Senate that similar cries of regimentation and totalitarianism had been raised in opposition to Abraham Lincoln's campaign for internal improvements, to the income tax, to the Federal Reserve Act, to the regulation of stock exchanges and to the legalization of collective bargaining rights by the Wagner Labor Relations Act.

The second argument was that continuing full employment would be undesirable because:

1. It would be inflationary.
2. It would deny boom-and-bust profits to those large companies that have learned to "ride the business bicycle" by picking up depression bargains and forcing small competitors to the wall.
3. It would deny employers the protection of a "floating number of unemployed," thereby enlarging working people's bargaining power.
4. With jobs for all, people would be less interested in working.
5. The most government should do is prevent mass depression.

The committee majority countered these views by insisting that:

1. Under conditions of continuing full employment, government, business, and labor could prevent inflation without regimentation and remove one of the causes of inflation itself—namely, the fear of recession or depression.
2. The lure of boom-and-bust profits has no place in civilized society.
3. A "safe pool of unemployed" undermines the market for the output of business.
4. Low productivity, featherbedding, and the stretch-out are promoted by job insecurity and unemployment, not by full employment.
5. "The belief that the prevention of mass unemployment is sufficient is merely another echo of the defeatist dogma that full employment is impossible under our economic system."

The third argument was that the government's responsibility should be limited to the relief of destitution. Thus, Rufus Tucker, chief economist of the General Motors Corporation, argued that providing relief would be cheaper than maintaining full employment. And Ira Mosher, president of the National Association of Manufacturers, argued that instead of full employment, we should be ready to meet depression with a strictly limited combination of home relief, work relief, and public works.

In response, the committee majority argued that full employment would be cheaper than relief in economic terms and much more beneficial in social terms. While not opposing a relief program for those unable to work, they favored instead the provision of useful jobs at fair rates of compensation, and opposed the idea of making relief or public works the first line of defense against depression or recession.

But the committee's majority did not win its case on all these points. Essentially, the 1946 statute's major contribution was to make the historic commitment that no further mass depression would be tolerated. And it is important to note that since its enactment there has been no depression, no near-depression, and, at least until the present, no threat of depression. In turn, this situation in America has tended to bolster the markets of the other advanced capitalist countries where there likewise has been no depression, no near-depression and, at least until now, no threat of depression. This was the great compromise embodied in the Employment Act of 1946. Its corollary, of course, as indicated in the testimony of the General Motors economist quoted above, has been the expansion of relief rolls as a substitute for jobs.

A NEW ECONOMIC BRINKMANSHIP

Many of us who fought the old battle against mass depression thought that the Age of the Dinosaur was gone forever. The new giant corporation, we wanted to believe, was more enlightened. Some of us, like Carl Keysen, discovered it had a soul. Some of us saw it as the fountainhead of efficiency, the torchbearer of progress, and the new voice of social responsibility. Because it was far better served by technicians, experts, and managers than any prewar corporation, some—like Daniel Bell and John K. Galbraith—hailed the withering away of the capitalist class and saluted the new rule of the experts, that is, people like themselves . . . and ourselves.

In one sense, they were right. The old dinosaurs did wither away. They have been replaced by a new generation of dinosaurs, each served by a glittering and well-paid retinue of fellow traveling lawyers, accountants, media wizards, senators, representatives, U.S. presidents and vice-presidents, public officials, computer pundits, and deep-thinking swamis from Harvard, Yale, Columbia, and Chicago.

The new dinosaurs, to their eternal credit, never repeat the vulgar "Marxism" of their predecessors: they never hold that depressions are inevitable under capitalism and are the price "we" pay for the maintenance of private enterprise. Their nervous systems are well attuned to the acceptance of whatever volume of government guarantees and subsidies may be required to maintain their markets, expand their cash flows, subsidize their export of capital to other countries, and prevent a depression in their own affairs.

But recessions are something else. For many of the supergiant multinational corporations, a recession is a pause that refreshes. Charles Levinson points out in his book Capital, Inflation and the Multinationals (Macmillan, 1971):

> For modern firms that have expanded at a fast clip, a
> pause usually provides a breathing space in which to trim
> off marginal activities, discontinue slow-moving products
> and transfer assets out of less profitable operations. . . .
> Pulling off mergers, buying up majority or minority par-
> ticipations in foreign firms, forming joint ventures, creat-
> ing overseas distribution chains, etc., . . . many of these
> activities are, indeed, best achieved during downturns,
> when the objects of takeovers and amalgamations are short
> of capital and find it difficult to sustain sales . . . (p. 44).

But no public relations firm worthy of its tax-deductible govern-ment-subsidized fees would allow direct reference to these or any other activities to maximize corporate money making. Rather, we hear that increased unemployment, even as officially underestimated, is unavoidable, that we must grin and bear it as a way of curbing in-flation. Indeed, since 1969, "planned recession" has from time to time been the official policy of the various administrations and of the Federal Reserve system. The essential view of both has been rather frankly stated by Professor Walter Grinder of Rutgers: "It's not that we look favorably upon depressions or recessions. It's just that they are necessary after a bout of antisocial overinvestment in capital, en-gendered by expansionary monetary policy" (Business Week, August 3, 1974, p. 41). True, on October 9, 1974, Gerald Ford stood in his rose garden and said "I do not think the United States is in a recession." On the following day, fortunately, William Safire, former speech writer for Richard Nixon, translated Ford's double-talk into plain English. At the time Ford's "calculated policy," wrote Safire, was

> not only to deny the existence of the present recession but
> to steadfastly assert he will not tolerate a recession in the
> future. . . . Of course, no sane political figure is going to
> say a kind word for recession—but the universally avoided
> truth is that there is at present no better way to increase
> productivity in plants, to turn impulse buyers into careful
> shoppers at supermarkets, and to cut seriously into rising
> living costs. (New York Times, October 10, 1974)

In return for such frankness, the most that Walter Grinder or Safire can expect is that upon application the White House will mail them WIN buttons for their lapels. Grinder will never climb into the big league swami circle at Harvard or Chicago unless he learns how to juggle reports on "demand pulls," "cost pushes," and conversations with his favorite computer. As for Safire, if he could only invent new catchwords to explain that Ford is "whipping inflation now" by cutting social services, by raising military expenditures, by providing advance pardons to polluters, and by giving gifts to the Rockefellers through enlarged tax exemptions for capital investment and dividends, then he might work himself back to the White House staff.

In favoring a "small" or "short-term" recession, the new dinosaurs and their fellow travelers are playing with an economic brinkmanship that would make John Foster Dulles look like a pacifist. Ford, Greenspan, Burns, and their banking-business supporters and sponsors blithely overlook the possibility that the deepening and extension of the present recession could get out of hand. Under current international conditions, a deeper or more extended recession in this country could plunge the economies of Western Europe and Japan—all of whom are far more dependent on American markets than Arab oil—into a catastrophe, and that would quickly boomerang on us. That is why so many European leaders are looking nervously at the wild men in the White House and praying that someone will put a little sense into their heads.

Hiding Unemployment

If my remarks seem to suggest that the history of old-time opposition to full employment is repeating itself, let me correct that impression. There is a major difference, as Bell and Galbraith have repeatedly informed us. Now, as distinguished from then, we are blessed with "knowledge elites" who dominate a "technostructure" that does all sorts of nice things. One of these, Bell tells us, is the fine tuning of the economy. Another, Galbraith announces in The New Industrial State (1968), is "a high standard of personal honesty," inasmuch as "the technostructure does not permit of the privacy that misfeasance and malfeasance require" (p. 128). Since the Bell and Galbraith revelations both went to the printer before the advent of high-rise stagflation and the corporation-financed Watergate horrors, let us overlook these matters and turn instead to two of the less advertised achievements of the knowledge elites.

The first is the fantastic progress over the past 30 years in the dubious arts of undercounting the unemployed and underemployed. The dinosaurs of 30 years ago could object to full employment because the idea (and the reality during World War II) smacked of a labor shortage. But the new dinosaurs of today can easily embrace the words "full employment" when their fellow travelers or hired hands have redefined the term to mean a labor surplus. This remarkable statistical shell game operates at many levels:

1. Defining full employment as a "tolerable" level of unemployment, first 2 to 3 to 4 percent or a narrowly defined labor force and then narrowing still further the definition of the labor force and raising the level of toleration to 5 and 6 percent.

2. Keeping from public attention the government's findings that 4 to 5 percent of officially defined unemployment in an average month means that 15 to 16 percent of the labor force is officially unemployed at some time during the same year.

3. Keeping from public attention the government's findings that of the adults not in the labor force, there are more people not working who "want work now" than the certified job seekers, that is, the officially unemployed.

4. Pretending that most people on relief do not want to work and that they have to be forced to accept nonexistent positions at decent wages.

5. Refusing to allow any serious survey of the work capabilities and desires of all those in the country's potential labor supply with all that this means for the continuing undercount of the "keep-outs," "push-outs," and "dropouts" from the so-called labor force.

6. Appointing a new statistical commission to cover up the past cover-ups and respond to the wave of recent criticisms by developing new ways of hiding unemployment and using the words "full employment" to disguise the waste of human resources.

Hiding Profits

The second achievement, while less mentionable in polite circles, is much more important: namely, the cover-up of money maximization by the multinational giants in banking, industry, agribusiness, services, and the media.

During World War II, when war mobilization created widespread shortages of raw materials, capital goods, and consumer goods, it was obvious that these shortages provided some powerful corporations with fantastic opportunities for making money by following the good old maxim: "Charge the most the market will bear, plus 10 percent." Many of these opportunities continued during the period after the war; indeed, new ones were created by the huge backlog of effective demand for consumer goods. In both those periods, one factor was obvious: unrestrained corporate money making in all its many forms (profiteering, speculation, quality gouging, payoffs on public contracts, cost plus contracts, etc.) was an important factor in inflationary trends. I am not suggesting that either economists or public officials were very elegant in analyzing the nature of money maximization, which has always involved capital accumulation not only through profits but also through all the other modes of property income: interest, rent, dividends, capital gains, and so on. Indeed, while some officials in the so-called regulatory commissions tried to cope with all of these complex forms, economists rose above the complexity. For the most part, they glibly used "profits" to refer to any and all forms of property income and, to compound the felony, as in the typical economics textbook, completely ignored the way in which accounting firms calculate profits in either reports to the Treasury Department or to the investing public. Nonetheless, it was at least respectable to talk about unrestrained profit seeking as a factor in inflation and business-cycle psychology.

Since then a tremendous change has taken place in the money-maximizing capabilities of modern corporate giants. The huge conglomerates have escaped the narrow confines of products and sectors; they have learned how to make money by making or doing anything. The hugh multinationals have transcended the confines of their domestic bases; they have learned how to make money anyplace. They have learned to make money by rigging stock markets in many countries and juggling international currencies. They have learned how to milk the public treasuries of many countries by plush and unsupervised government contracts, by myriad tax havens well designed to take the risk out of money maximization and brilliantly described by their public relations departments as "incentives to risk taking" and by low-interest government loans to bail them out whenever they get into trouble. They have escaped the fly-by-night, get-rich-quick mentality of their predecessors and have developed 5, 10, 15, and 20 year plans for globe-girdling capital expansion. The banking multinationals have learned how to raise their prices (namely, interest rates) to unprecedented heights, using innumerable variants of the old shrill cry, "What's good for Chase Manhattan is good for all the

world." The nonbanking multinationals have learned how to respond
to either rising interest rates, declining demand or both by upping
their prices in order to enlarge their cash flows and thereby provide
the capital for future expansion. Together, these remarkable money-
maximizing institutions have learned how to exploit the money-making
potentialities of every shortage of oil, food, or any other commodity
anyplace in the world and of every drought or other natural disaster.
And when adequate supplies or a genuine surplus threatens to curtail
prices or profits—as in the case of oil—they have learned how to curtail production, hide inventories, destroy supplies, promote waste,
fight conservation, or even, in certain cases, to manufacture artificial
shortages. Indeed, the banking and nonbanking multinationals have
whipped up such an orgy of inflationary price increases that the danger
of imminent worldwide collapse may well be around the corner.

All of this seems to have required a lowering of visibility. And
so we find at least three forms of cover-up. First, at the micro level
of the individual conglomerate or multinational, the typical corporate
balance sheet is like a costume at a masquerade ball: what it reveals
is minimal. The same is true of corporate reports to the Internal
Revenue Service, except that the latter tend to conceal taxable profits
and assets and the former have tended to reveal a steadily rising
earning per share in order to stimulate the demand for shares. In
either case, the profits and earnings figures are far from being objective facts. Rather, they are the designed outcome of creative and
artful juggling in calculating the cost of withdrawals from inventory,
estimating depreciation, pushing revenues and costs forward or backward in time, capitalizing operating expenditures, and juggling the
accounts of subsidiaries and subsidiaries of subsidiaries. This is a
game not merely for certified public accountants (who usually perform
well for the people who pay them) but also for tax lawyers, and cooperative generals, admirals, and civilian bureaucrats in public agencies.

Second, at the macro level, national economic accounting supplies a macro-economic cover-up. On the one hand, the corporate
profit figures are huge aggregates, bringing together those companies
with the highest reported profits and those with the lowest. With this
kind of disaggregated calculation it would be entirely possible for the
national accounts to show (in classically Marxian terms) a "declining
rate of profit" for all reporting corporations at a time when a few
dominant multinationals are making more money than ever before.[5]
On the other hand, the national economic accounts are even less reliable than the masquerade balance sheets since their profit data are
based on corporate reports to the Internal Revenue Service, themselves the product of artful and high-priced manipulations by accountants and lawyers instructed to hide taxable profits and minimize

long-run taxable income and assets. Since I assume that they are
usually successful in carrying out their instructions, I am always
amazed by the way in which most economists—liberals and radicals
as well as conservatives—seem to take them at face value.

Third, there is the supermodern school of thought, led by Galbraith, which describes the modern corporate giant—the most highly
organized money maker in history—as an institution no longer interested in money maximization. This remarkable tour de force is ac-
complished by a false distinction between a corporation's economic
growth and its profit making or profitability. Galbraith naively discusses a corporation's growth as though it somehow or other had no
direct connection with the corporation's efforts to attain a long-term
maximization of cash flow and all other forms of money power. Still
more naively, he discusses profits in the narrow technical sense of
dividends to stockholders rather than in the broader sense of capital
accumulation available for all who can get their fingers into the pot,
whether managers or stockholders. In the course of demonstrating
his almost limitless naivete, Galbraith informs us that the giant corporation is the guarantor of technical progress, thereby thrusting
aside decades of evidence that many corporate giants hold back new
technologies in order to maximize profitability. His claim, mentioned
above, that the giant corporation's "high standard of personal honesty," thrives because "the technostructure does not permit the privacy that misfeasance and malfeasance require" sounds very strange
today in light of the misfeasance and malfeasance at Franklin National
Bank, Penn Central, and Equity Funding, not to mention the business
contributors behind the Watergate scandals and scores of other huge
companies involved in tangled webs of corporate and personal dishon-
esty. "Why punish these men?" asked a defense lawyer back in the
early 1960s when 28 General Electric executives were sentenced for
price-rigging. "It's a way of life. Everybody's doing it."[6] If we accepted Galbraith's story, we would have to believe nobody's been doing it.

As a result of all these cover-ups, corporate money making is
rarely discussed as something related to the present worldwide inflation. It is polite, even wise, to find the sources of inflation in "cost
pushes," "demand pulls," or "unavoidable shortages," to use the
terminology of a liberal from Yale's economics department. But it is
no longer polite to include among the costs the costs of capital: i.e.,
profits, interest, rents, capital gains, or any form of property income.
"Costs" means wage costs, even though it is obvious that wages have
been lagging far behind price increases. And this at a time when even
the openly reported profits of American and Western oil corporations,
both on imported oil and on domestic oil, have reached fabulous
heights! Nor is it polite to include in "demand pull" the insatiable

corporate demand for additional capital to be exported all over the
world. "Demand" is now limited to the unpleasant aftermath of spending money for welfare, food stamps, public health, or a few more public service jobs. And as for "shortages," they are all made by Nature, God, or the godless Arabs—never, never contrived, enlarged, or
even prolonged by the corporations that, by simple good luck, happen
to profit from them.

THE NEW STRUCTURE OF BUSINESS POWER

If I have been somewhat ungenerous toward the media stars of
economic policy, let me now concede the enormous difficulties that
anyone faces in trying to understand the current realities of economic
policy making. In this rapidly changing era it is not only unemployment and money accumulation that are covered up but the structure
of business power itself. In all the countries of the developed world,
modern capitalism has been undergoing vast changes since the end of
World War II. These are too complex and profound to review at this
time. But in considering the relation between a genuine full employment program and American business, it would be the height of folly
to think that the American business system can be represented by
Adam Smith's model of perfect competition or by the new variations
of this myth used in the computerized models of Keynesian macroeconomists. These computers have a human failing: they too can be
brainwashed. And generally they have been. Their electronic brains
have been programmed in such a way as to completely ignore, or re-
ject, any and all relevant information on the planning, programming,
and price-setting power of the new multinational, conglomerate banking and industrial corporations that operate on a global basis with no
particular allegiance to any market (i.e., nation state) in which they
operate.

Of course, this is not the whole of the American economy, and,
indeed, as I have already suggested, there is less and less reason to
regard the American-based multinationals as American per se. If
they can make more money by upsetting the American currency or
economy, that's too bad—it's a problem for the public relations department. "The mere spot on which they stand," to quote Thomas
Jefferson in reference to the merchant kings of an earlier era, "does
not constitute so strong an attachment as that from which they draw
their gains."[7] Because ITT has many countries, it has no country . . .

But the American economic structure is not limited to the multinationals. Whether one looks at it in terms of labor markets, of
production sectors, or of power structures, the picture is enormously

complex. In 1971, Peter Doeringer and Michael Piore, with help from many others, formulated the dual labor market theory, which made a sharp distinction between the capital-intensive, largely unionized sector of large-scale oligopolistic planners and the labor-intensive, less-unionized, low-wage and highly competitive small business sector.[8] Two years later Galbraith picked up this idea, and emphasizing the employers' role more than the employees', presented it as his theory of an American economy divided into two parts, the planning system and the market system.[9] Recognizing the absurdity of subsuming the entire public sector under big business oligopoly, James O'Connor then raised the ante from two to three by accepting the dual labor market or Galbraithean dichotomy but adding on the public sector for separate treatment.[10] More recently, S. M. Miller has pointed out that medium-sized business is more important in terms of employment (as contrasted with assets, gains, or power) than either big or small business, and has special cultural and political orientations.[11] This gives us four separate, although closely intertwined, sectors of output, and four separate, although interconnected, labor markets. And if we focus on labor markets as distinguished from output sectors, I think it also necessary to separate out the special market for professional, technical, and scientific services, a market that cuts horizontally across the four output sectors. In this fifth labor market, which includes academic workers as well as lawyers, accountants, and others, we find entirely different patterns of certification, recruitment, career advancement, job tenure, and wage policies. It is this fivefold complexity which makes increasingly ridiculous any effort to develop national economic policies based on the premise that all trends in demand, supply, factor returns, and prices are identical. Under the Hawkins-Humphrey Job Guarantee Bill, as I understand it, the full employment program would deal not only with the aggregate demand for and supply of labor but also in disaggregated terms with every major program area. In so dealing, I believe it would be of enormous help in preserving the small- and medium-sized business sectors. It would also help civilize those multinational companies that have lost contact with America and seem to operate on the principle that worldwide giantism in capital accumulation is the highest virtue, and extremism in the pursuit of money is no sin.

Realism tells us, however, that a genuine full employment program, as envisioned in the Hawkins-Humphrey measure, is scarcely feasible in the United States if it is confronted with the complete opposition of business leadership. Of all sectors of business oppose a comprehensive program of genuine full employment without inflation, the program will be rejected by Congress, approved with crippling amendments, or slaughtered in the back alleys of the White House and departmental bureaucracies. Certainly, the Employment Act of 1946 would never have become law if it had not enjoyed rather enthusiastic support from many businesses in the small and medium sectors, as well as more modulated support from rather enlightened big business associated with the Committee for Economic Development and the National Planning Association. As one looks back on the kind of business leadership exercised 30 years ago, one is tempted to ask, "Where are the Paul Hoffmans of yesteryear? Where are today's counterparts of Taussig, Stimson, Stettinius, Benton, Bowles, and Flanders?"

One answer, I suppose, is that the Nixon administration developed the kind of business-government partnership that brought out the worst in big business leadership, rewarding business executives for suppressing any inclinations toward moderating their extremism in the pursuit of money. Now that Nixon is gone and Nixonism a little weaker, there is a likelihood that a new breed of business leadership will emerge. I see this likelihood because I believe that genuine and sustained full employment without inflation or war is possible under capitalism.

Back in 1945, my old friend and colleague Gerhard Colm discussed this definitively. A grandfather was telling his grandson, Colm wrote, the story of an alligator chasing a frog. The frog jumped from the log into the river, swam through the river, hopped on land—the alligator coming closer and closer. When the alligator finally cornered the frog under a tree and opened its mouth to swallow the frog, things were getting desperate for both frog and storyteller. The old man knew only one solution: "The frog looked up and saw the tree and just as the 'gator's jaws were closing down, the frog flew up into the tree." "But Grandpa," said the little boy, "frogs can't fly." "Indeed, they cain't, Son, indeed, they cain't," was the answer, "but this frog flew—he had to."[12]

Neither Gerhard Colm nor Leon Keyserling nor any of the others who helped that frog fly were thanked for their work. Indeed, during the entire New Deal-Fair Deal period few of those who helped save American capitalism were praised for their efforts. The tendency, rather, was to pillory them as "eggheads," "pinkoes," and advocates of "creeping socialism." Franklin Roosevelt himself was branded a "traitor to his class" and died as the worst hated as well as the best loved of all presidents.

Today, I suspect, the jaws of the alligator are getting closer. The entire system could yet be caught in the grip of worldwide recession and inflation. But the threat of imminent crisis is not enough. Nor will the crisis itself be enough to provoke a creative response. Courageous leadership is required. On the political front such courage has been shown by Augustus Hawkins, Hubert Humphrey, and their 65 cosponsors of the proposed legislation. It is being shown by the many senators and members of Congress who are preparing new breakthrough legislation in such vital fields as day care, housing, mass transportation, health services, tax reform, the control of oligopolistic price fixing by business, and the control of the Federal Reserve system. But they need help from many, many sources. Above all, from the academic community, from teachers, researchers, and students who are willing to transcend the sterilizing constraints of accepted economics and deal creatively with all of the political, social, cultural, and moral—as well as economic—requirements of a society more squarely based on the recognition of all human rights and the guaranteeing of the rights of all adults to "equal opportunities for useful paid employment at fair rates of compensation."

NOTES

1. The War Contracts Subcommittee of the Senate Military Affairs Committee.

2. Arthur S. Miller, "Legal Foundations of the Corporate State," Journal of Economic Issues, March 1972, p. 68.

3. Additional material on this change may be found in Bertram M. Gross and Jeffrey D. Straussman, "Full Employment Growthmanship and the Expansion of Labor Supply," The Annals, March 1975.

4. U.S. Congress, Senate, Assuring Full Employment in a Free Competitive Economy, 79th Cong., 1st sess., Senate Report 583. Reprinted together with Minority Report in Senate Committee on Labor and Public Welfare, History of Employment and Manpower Policy in the United States (Washington, D.C.: U.S. Government Printing Office, 1965), pp. 2390-2431.

5. This is the fallacy of the "declining rate of profit" argument in Andrew Glyn and Bob Sutcliffe, Capitalism in Crisis (New York: Pantheon, 1972), which presents a neo-Marxian picture of declining profitability for British business.

6. As quoted in Ovid Demaris, Dirty Business: The Corporate-Political Money-Power Game (New York: Harpers Magazine Press, 1974), p. 10.

7. Letter from Thomas Jefferson to Horatio G. Spafford, March 17, 1814.

8. Peter B. Doeringer and Michael J. Piore, Internal Labor Markets and Manpower Analysis (Lexington, Mass.: Heath, 1971).

9. John K. Galbraith, Economics and the Public Purpose (Boston: Houghton Mifflin, 1973).

10. James O'Connor, The Fiscal Crisis of the State (New York: St. Martin's, 1973).

11. In an unpublished manuscript, Miller estimates civilian, non-agricultural employment in 1973 as follows: big business, 17.5 million (21.7 percent); medium business, 30.0 million (37.3 percent); small business, 15.4 million (19.2 percent); public and nonprofit, 17.5 million (21.7 percent).

12. Gerhard Colm, "Maintaining High-Level Production and Employment: A Symposium," American Political Science Review, December 1945.

3

RECONSIDERING
EMPLOYMENT POLICY
Charles C. Killingsworth

Less than 10 years ago, Time magazine celebrated the triumph of the "new economics" by featuring John Maynard Keynes on its cover. In 1966, Robert Lekachman published the Age of Keynes, and Daniel Fusfeld enlarged the theme with The Age of the Economist. With the major problems involved in maintaining full employment, price stability, and economic growth presumably solved, discussion turned increasingly to techniques for "fine tuning"—that is, ways to control even minor deviations from the desired economic performance.

Today it appears that the decade of the 1960s was the Keynesian Camelot. Talk of fine tuning the economy is a bitter joke when economists appear to have no answers, or at least no consensus on answers, to the unprecedented conjunction of double-digit inflation, falling gross national product, and rapidly rising unemployment. President Nixon voiced a generally recognized truth when he told a press conference in 1973, "My economic advisers are not always right, but they are always sure in everything that they recommend."[1] The September 30, 1974 issue of Newsweek contained a special economic report which had as one of its themes the current general disillusionment with macroeconomics and economists. A fairly typical quotation was one from Nobel laureate Wassily Leontief: "The macroeconomists work by disregarding details. . . . There's a lot of fancy methodology, but the macroeconomists get indigestion if you give them facts. . . . Their systems didn't perform as expected." Not long after, Nat Goldfinger, research director for the AFL-CIO and president of the Industrial Relations Research Association, delivered a broader indictment:

─────────

Originally published in Social Policy 5, no. 5 (January/February 1975), pp. 13-19. © 1975 by Social Policy Corporation.

That whole crew of academic economists, from the conservative types to the liberal types, have been proven
utterly wrong over the past two or three years, at least,
and I would say, for an even longer period of time. In
fact, one of the difficulties in the American economic
situation today . . . is the bankruptcy of the academic
economic establishment . . .2

One CBS News documentary on inflation completely omitted any inter-
views with economists. Why? "Frankly, that would be confusing,"
was the answer.

With economic policy now in fairly general disarray, it is vital
to analyze what went wrong. The first step in building a new conceptual foundation for economic policy is to understand the significant
weaknesses in the old foundation. My thesis here is that the macroeconomists fell into error primarily because they grossly misinterpreted what was happening in the U.S. economy, especially in the labor
market, during the latter half of the 1960s, and that this misinterpretation led them to a gross overestimate of the power of fiscal and
monetary policy. There were subsidiary errors that flowed from this
basic one, and which should be analyzed, but I will give them only
passing attention here.

CREEPING PROSPERITY UNEMPLOYMENT

To understand this basic error of interpretation, it is necessary
to return to the early 1960s controversy as to whether inadequacy of
aggregate demand or structural change in the economy was responsible for excessive prosperity unemployment. The setting for this debate was a kind of stair-step rise in average national unemployment
rates during each of the prosperity periods after 1950. In the first of
these periods, including and following the Korean War, the average
unemployment rate was at or below 3 percent. During the prosperity
period of 1955-57, unemployment was at or a little above 4 percent.
After the 1958 recession, the prosperity level of unemployment was
about 5 percent. And after the 1959-60 recession, unemployment remained at or a little above 5.5 percent.

The Council of Economic Advisers under Kennedy was the leading proponent of the view that the basic cause of "creeping prosperity
unemployment," as it was sometimes called, was a chronic inadequacy
of "aggregate demand"—that is, total expenditures by government,
businesses, and individuals. This inadequacy in turn was attributed
primarily to "fiscal drag," which was explained as the tendency of the

federal income tax to generate revenues during an economic expansion
at a more rapid rate than federal expenditures increased. Thus, pro-
gressivity in the tax system acted as a drag on the economy during
periods of expansion, slowing and then stopping growth well short of
the potential of the economy. Theoretically this drag could be offset
by cutting federal income taxes, or by increasing federal expenditures,
or by some combination of both. In practice the Kennedy council favored cutting taxes.[3]

The aggregate demand diagnosis and policy prescription rested
upon a distinctive view of markets in general and the labor market in
particular that was articulated somewhat later in the 1960s. Two il-
lustrations will be sufficient to characterize the viewpoint. Walter
Heller, chairman of the Kennedy council, wrote in 1966:

> It is often said that the study of economics makes people
> conservative. In the microeconomic sense, it undoubtedly
> does. It is hard to study the modern economics of rela-
> tive prices, resource allocation, and distribution without
> developing a healthy respect for the market mechanism on
> three major scores: first, for what Robert Dorfman calls
> its "cybernetics," for the incredible capacity of the price
> system to receive and generate information and respond
> to it; second, for its technical efficiency and hardheaded-
> ness as a guide to resources and a goad to effort and risk-
> taking; and third, for its contribution to political democ-
> racy by keeping economic decisions free and decentralized.[4]

Like the good academician that he is, Heller immediately added, "I do
not carry respect to the point of reverence," and specified some
shortcomings of "the market mechanism." Also in 1966, the report
of what was popularly called the Automation Commission was issued.
In general, the analytical parts of this report followed rather closely
the doctrines of the new economics. One significant passage read:

> It is the proper function of a market to allocate resources,
> and in this respect the labor market does not function dif-
> ferently from any other. If the available resources are of
> high quality, the market will adjust to the use of high quali-
> ty resources; if the quality is low, methods will be devel-
> oped to use such resources. . . . In a slack labor market
> employers must have some means of selecting among
> numerous applicants, and it is not surprising that edu-
> cational attainment is often used as a convenient yard-
> stick, regardless of its direct relevance to the require-
> ments of the job.

We have found it useful to view the labor market as a gigantic "shape-up" with members of the labor force queued in order of their relative attractiveness to employers. . . . The total number employed and unemployed depends primarily on the general state of economic activity. The employed tend to be those near the beginning and the unemployed those near the end of the line. Only as demand rises will employers reach further down the line in their search for employees. . . . And because workers of low educational attainment are the least desirable to employers, nonwhite and older workers are concentrated at the rear of the line, not only because of their lower educational attainment, but also because of direct discrimination.[5]

Although these views had not been articulated as fully in the early 1960s, they were assumed implicitly in the policy positions taken by the new economics. Thus tax cutting was embraced as the preferred form of fiscal stimulus. Heller and others, mainly in retrospect, expressed some nostalgic preference for increased government expenditures, but when tax cutting came to appear to be more expedient politically, the new economics seemed to have little difficulty in adapting to that form of fiscal stimulus. It seems not unjustified to suggest that "healthy respect"—though not reverence—for the market mechanism of the private sector may have made tax cutting reasonably palatable to the new economics. Cutting taxes reduces, at least relatively, the government-controlled sector of the economy and enlarges the market-controlled sector. And that helps to capture the conservative vote.

The new economics insisted that there had been no weakening of market mechanisms and no structural changes in the economy that had contributed to the development of excessive unemployment. Therefore, this view ran, it should be obvious that fiscal and monetary policy alone, working on aggregate demand, would be sufficient to reduce unemployment to the "interim target" of 4 percent. Before that level was achieved, the new economics taught, human-power training and other forms of labor market intervention could contribute but little to the reduction of the average level of unemployment.[6]

The competing explanation for creeping prosperity unemployment was generally known as the structuralist viewpoint, usually referred to in quotation marks and frequently distorted.[7] The essence of this viewpoint was that fiscal drag and chronic inadequacy of aggregate demand were indeed real and serious problems which had contributed to high levels of prosperity unemployment, but they were far from the whole story, and demand expansion, while part of the solution, was not enough by itself. This group argued that some basic structural changes had occurred in the economy since World War II which had reduced the job opportunities for less skilled and less educated workers while increasing them for more skilled and better educated workers. The massive decline in agricultural employment and the massive growth of employment in the professions were cited as examples. The labor market was simply not powerful or efficient enough to correct the resulting imbalances without some new forms of social intervention, and a pure and simple increase in aggregate demand would not change the growth patterns of the economy sufficiently to offset these new imbalances. Without large-scale humanpower and labor market policy initiatives to complement fiscal stimulus, the structuralists argued, tax cutting was not likely to reduce prosperity level unemployment much below 5 percent.[8]

"THE GREAT EXPERIMENT"

The sequel to that debate can hardly be regarded as an untold story. An enormous tax cut was enacted early in 1964, with further, smaller, reductions provided for 1965. Presumably the country was about to see a rare phenomenon: the practical testing of a basic economic theory. Would the fiscal stimulus of the tax cuts, aided only by the appropriate monetary policies, achieve full employment? Thus the issue seemed to be posed. And to many well-known economists, the answer has seemed to be perfectly clear.

The Automation Commission was among the first to give its interpretation of the outcome of this "great experiment":

> When Public Law 88-444 was passed [August 1964], the national unemployment rate was 5.1 percent. As this report is finished [February 1966] it is 4.0 percent. The experience of the economy during the life of this Commission is the best evidence that economic growth can continue to offset the growth of productivity and labor force and reduce unemployment further.[9]

Paul Samuelson offered the following assessment in his Newsweek column in 1969:

> Charles Killingsworth, Norbert Wiener, Michael Harrington and other prophets of an automation revolution were sure ten years ago that "structural unemployment" was America's main problem. Robert Solow and other Kennedy

advisers made econometric estimates to show that expansionary fiscal and monetary policies would melt the hard core of unemployment and that little of the excess unemployment that prevailed in 1961 was structural and new. Again, events proved that macroeconomics can, black youths aside, achieve full employment.[10]

In a book published in 1974, James Tobin followed his misstatement of the structuralist position with:

One of the first tasks we set ourselves at the Council was to refute this diagnosis. Our refutation . . . was gloriously confirmed by the ease with which new jobs were created and unemployment diminished in the subsequent expansion of aggregate demand.[11]

Many other proponents of the new economics, including Walter Heller and Gardner Ackley, have written in the same vein, which Lester Thurow summed up in this way: "The history of the 1960s demonstrated that the American economy can reach unemployment rates of close to 3 percent through the use of simple fiscal and monetary policies."[12] The same lesson was drawn from this experiment in the United States by many foreign observers,[13] and it is now part of the conventional wisdom that simple fiscal and monetary policy has the power to drive the U.S. unemployment rate well below the 4 percent level.

When the large tax cut of 1964 was passed, the national unemployment rate was 5.5 percent. By 1968, the rate was 3.6 percent, and in 1969 it was 3.5 percent. In no small measure, these simple numbers and the interpretation placed on them by the great majority of economists were the basis for the high regard enjoyed by the new economics in the late 1960s.

BEYOND FISCAL AND MONETARY POLICY

The foregoing interpretation embodies a familiar kind of fallacy identified as post hoc ergo propter hoc: because b happens after a happens, b must be caused by a. The unstated, and unexamined, assumption in this case is that only "simple fiscal and monetary policies" caused the decrease in the national unemployment rate after 1964.

I am tempted to sermonize about how alarming it is that so many reputable economists relied so heavily on such a simplistic

assumption without any apparent effort to check on its validity. But it
may be more useful to point out the significant factors other than simple fiscal and monetary policies that reduced the reported national
unemployment rate after 1964. As I have described these other factors in considerable detail elsewhere,[14] a relatively brief summary
will suffice.

First, there were two changes in the definition of unemployment—one in early 1965, and the other in early 1967. The first involved a change in the labor force classification of enrollees in certain kinds of human-power programs. Historically, most such
enrollees had been counted as unemployed; for example, in the unemployment statistics of the 1930s, WPA workers were part of the
unemployed total. Beginning early in 1965, enrollees in the Neighborhood Youth Corps, the College Work-Study program, and some other
similar work-relief programs were counted as employed. A conservative estimate of the effect of this definition change is that it reduced
the national unemployment rate by as much as 0.5 percent by the late
1960s.[15] The second change in definition involved dropping persons
less than 16 years old from the labor force statistics and tightening
the definition of "seeking work," among other things. The Bureau of
Labor Statistics has estimated that this change, or set of changes, reduced the reported national unemployment rate by 0.2 percent.[16]
Therefore, if the pre-1965 definitions had been applied after 1965,
the reported unemployment rates would have been at least 0.7 percent higher in the later 1960s. Put another way, the changes reduced
the reported rate by at least 0.7 percent.

Second, the size of the armed forces was substantially increased
starting in 1965, and draft deferment policies resulted in increased
college enrollments by young men, starting in the fall of 1965. By
relatively conservative estimating methods, I have concluded that the
net effect of this factor by 1969 was a reduction in the reported national unemployment rate of approximately 0.5 percent. Using a different estimating method, Geoffrey Moore of the National Bureau of
Economic Research has concluded that the reduction in the unemployment rate from this cause was in the range of 0.6 to 0.7 percent.[17]

The two factors discussed above obviously fall outside the realm
of simple fiscal and monetary policy. The magnitude of their effects
can certainly be estimated with as much accuracy as many other economic variables which are routinely estimated. There is no "double
counting." In the absence of these factors, the reported national unemployment rate would have been from 1.2 percent to 1.4 percent
higher than it was in 1968 and 1969. In other words, the reported rate
would have been in the range of 4.8 to 5.0 percent in 1968, and 4.7 to
4.9 percent in 1969. In still other words, simple fiscal and monetary
policy alone would not have reduced the unemployment rate below

those figures. To attribute the entire reduction in unemployment rates after 1964 to simple fiscal and monetary policy is obviously to engage in gross exaggeration. That such exaggeration may result from fallacious reasoning rather than a conscious intent to mislead does not lessen the magnitude of the error.

One additional factor—sharply declining labor force participation rates among less educated men—also contributed to lower reported unemployment rates. This factor does not readily lend itself to precise quantification, and I will not attempt to present numerical estimates of its effect on the national unemployment rate. This approach is not intended to suggest that there was no effect on the numbers, because there obviously was a substantial effect. But this factor is more fruitfully treated, I believe, as an indicator of how the labor market was functioning during a period of high employment and low reported unemployment.

Between 1962 (a year of high reported unemployment rates) and 1969 (with 3.5 percent unemployment), there was a fairly general decline of labor force participation rates among men at all age levels with less than average education. Among most male age groups with more than average education, participation rates increased from 1962 to 1969. Within age groups, the lower the educational attainment, the greater the decline in participation. Generally, for groups showing such declines, they accelerated after 1967. While the declines were greater among the older and younger less educated men, they were surprisingly large even among men in the so-called prime ages—35 to 44 years. There were also large decreases in employment among the less educated men. Again, within age groups, the job losses were proportionately greater among the least educated. Generally, in these less educated groups, declining participation rates reduced the counted labor force somewhat more rapidly than jobs decreased, so that reported unemployment rates dropped. Despite this effect, the absolute unemployment rates generally remained substantially higher, at the end of the 1960s, for the less educated men than for the better educated men.[18] At the beginning of the decade, there were substantial average income differences between the better educated and the less educated men; by the end of the decade, the differences had widened even more.[19]

Thus, although the decade of the 1960s was a time of enormous increases in employment, the added jobs were not distributed in the way that the "queuing" or "shape-up" concept of the Automation Commission had implied they would be. The labor market did not induce employers to adapt their jobs to the capabilities of less educated workers, despite their much lower "price tags" and their much greater availability than the better educated group. Employers did not reach farther toward the rear of the hiring line for new hires;

instead, they competed with each other for the better educated workers who presumably stood near the head of the line. These better educated workers became increasingly scarce, and employers bid up their already high wage rates. At the far end of the line, jobs were disappearing, workers were dropping out of the line, and already low wage rates fell even lower relative to those at the head of the line. Economic growth did not offset the effects of structural changes which were reducing the demand for lower grades of labor at a somewhat faster rate than the supply of low skilled people was falling.

ECONOMICS AND REALITY

In the event that what I have said here will appear to some readers as a useless postmortem of a long-dead controversy, I must offer the viewpoint that those who fail to understand the past are condemned to repeat it. The half-truths of the doctrines of the new economics in the early 1960s led to the adoption of half-adequate policies. The gross misinterpretation of the behavior of the economy in the late 1960s led to grossly erroneous predictions of the effects of policies prescribed for the early 1970s, and to highly disappointing results from those policies. Now at mid-decade the credibility of economists both in and out of government has all but vanished. The first step in the reconstruction of economics as a reliable guide to effective policy must be to recognize what went wrong. The polity will continue to follow economic policies, good or bad, explicit or implicit; and an economics based more on reality and experience than on a priori doctrine may provide more reliable guides for policy than we have had in recent years.

The point can be illustrated by reference to a perhaps minor and certainly little-noticed disagreement in 1970. Late in 1969, the unemployment rate started rising rather sharply. Congress began consideration of a public service employment program to alleviate the unemployment. Herbert Stein, then chairman of the Council of Economic Advisers, opposed this program. In March 1970, he stated that the rise in unemployment was simply "transitional"—that is, a result of the winding down of the Vietnam war; therefore, he concluded, public service employment was an inappropriate remedy.[20] In the same month, in testimony before two congressional committees,[21] I predicted that the rising unemployment trend would continue (the rate then was 4.2 percent), that it would, at least, exceed 6 percent before declining, and that it would remain much higher than the levels of the late 1960s for an indefinite period. At about that time, the Council of Economic Advisers was still insisting that the average

unemployment rate for calendar 1970 would be 4.3 percent. The rate
reached 5 percent in July 1970, and continued up to slightly more than
6 percent. (The rate for calendar 1970 turned out to be 4.9 percent.)
In the 50 months since July 1970, the rate has been below 5 percent
in only 8 months, and never as low as 4.5 percent.

One of the rigorous tests of an economic model is its ability to
provide reasonably accurate predictions. Stein was relying on the basic model of the economy in general, and the labor market in particular,
that had been developed in the 1960s and which was described above.
This model provided highly inaccurate predictions; it also led to inappropriate and inadequate policy recommendations. I do not claim
perfection for my own model, but it is manifestly much closer to reality than Stein's was, as demonstrated by the much greater accuracy
of the predictions that I was able to make in 1970. It may be noted that
the public service employment program which Stein had opposed was
enacted by Congress late in 1970 and was vetoed by President Nixon.[22]
A somewhat watered-down version of the program was re-enacted by
Congress and reluctantly accepted by the administration in mid-1971,
when the unemployment rate had remained at roughly the 6 percent
level for more than six months.

At the possible risk of belaboring the obvious, I will briefly high-
light the basic differences between the Stein model and my own. Stein
apparently accepted the illusory view that the experience of the 1960s
demonstrated the ability of simple fiscal and monetary policy to push
the unemployment rate well below 4 percent. And he probably accepted
the corollary view that a period with more than 4 percent unemployment was necessary to check inflation, but thereafter signals could be
reversed and unemployment would fall.

My own view was that it was really the low unemployment rates
of the late 1960s that were transitional, and that the rise in unemployment which began late in 1969 represented the reappearance of the old
problems of the early 1960s. Those problems had been masked or de-
ferred, but not solved, by the definition changes of 1965 and 1967 and
by the effects of the Vietnam war. The persistence of high unemployment rates for nearly five years now should lend credence to that
view.

As already suggested, there were few substantial differences—
at least in the early years—between what came to be called Nixonomics and the new economics of the 1960s. As time passed, Nixonomics
placed more emphasis on inflation control and less on unemployment
reduction than the new economics had, but this was a difference in desired results (or trade-off) rather than a difference in basic models.
Indeed, early in 1971 Nixon himself was quoted as saying to a group
of news reporters that he was "now a Keynesian in economics."[23]

Tax cuts were proposed by the administration and passed by Congress in 1969 and 1970 when the economy slid into a recession, and the administration embraced the concept of the "full employment budget," which had been developed during the Democratic years of the 1960s. It was not until mid-1974 that this concept was explicitly renounced by the administration. For a time, the administration had been in the anomalous position of arguing that an unemployment rate somewhere between 4.5 and 5.0 percent represented full employment, while continuing to use the 4.0 percent figure for full employment budget purposes.

THE FLAWS IN THE BALANCING ACT

I asserted earlier that the basic error in interpreting the experience of the 1960s led to other errors. In concluding I will indicate briefly that I think they were.

The most obvious error was a great overestimate of the power of fiscal and monetary policy. The belief was that macroeconomics provided the answer not only to full employment but also to inflation control. If you could, solely by macroeconomic policies, achieve any desired unemployment rate goal (at least down to 3.5 percent), then you could also achieve any desired price stability goal. The widely discussed Phillips curve was thought to describe with reasonable precision the trade-off between unemployment and price stability; you had to buy price stability with higher unemployment, and lower unemployment with higher rates of price rise. The real problem was thought to be not how to achieve either goal, but how to strike a rational balance between them. For the past four or five years, of course, large budget deficits have failed to reduce unemployment significantly and high unemployment rates have failed to slow inflation.

A second error was a great overestimate of the power and efficiency of markets in general, and the labor market in particular. This mystique of the market (more prominent in Nixonomics than in the new economics, but present in both) led to: emphasis on tax cutting as the preferred form of fiscal stimulus; indefinite postponement of the time when "major attention" was recommended for programs of substantial social intervention in the labor market; prolonged and impassioned resistance to wage and price controls; halfhearted administration of those controls after they had become unavoidable; and premature loosening of the controls when they were beginning to show some encouraging results.

The doctrine that simple fiscal and monetary policy could easily drive the unemployment rate down to 4 percent, if not lower, led to the concept of the full employment budget according to which government revenues were estimated at what they would be if the economy were operating at a level consistent with 4 percent unemployment, and government expenditures were then planned according to that bench mark. To put the matter rather crudely, if expenditures came out to less than full employment revenues, the budget was considered to be "restrictive," and vice versa. Hence, tax cuts or more spending could be justified even if the budget was actually in deficit. The flaw in all of this, of course, is that simple fiscal and monetary policy cannot reduce unemployment to 4 percent. Therefore, fiscal policy has generally been substantially more stimulative than the 4 percent full employment budget implies. This fact undoubtedly helps to explain why fiscal policy has appeared to contribute so little to inflation control, even during the Nixon years.[24] We have had chronic overstimulation of the economy. It would be fatuous to blame Nixonomics for the oil crisis or worldwide crop failures. But these shocks to our economy and the price system would have had less impact if inflation had not already developed great momentum.

There is a serious danger in the present situation which may not be entirely obvious, at least to those who agree with my analysis. This danger is that the present disarray in economic policy may so thoroughly discredit macroeconomics that its basic teachings will be rejected or ignored by policy makers for years to come. Such an occurrence would seriously impede the development of an effective employment policy. I still believe, as I have been writing and testifying for many years, that effective fiscal and monetary policy is an indispensable part of an adequate employment policy. It was a mistake for the new economics to insist that fiscal and monetary policy had to be the first and the most important part of employment policy, and that only residual unemployment problems would require other kinds of treatment at some indefinite time in the future. Among other things, this mistake has stunted the development of human-power programs of a magnitude great enough to have a significant impact on the problems to which they are addressed. An obvious recent example is the public service employment program of 1971-72, which provided a grand total of about 180,000 job opportunities for 5 million unemployed, or a ratio of one job for each 27 job seekers.

Macroeconomics was so greatly oversold in the last decade that it has now lost almost all credibility with the informed public. While the deflation of excessive expectations is unavoidable and probably salubrious, complete rejection of macroeconomics because of the excesses of some of its practitioners could grow into one of the major problems in employment policy in the latter half of the 1970s.

NOTES

1. New York Times, October 4, 1973.

2. "Labor News Conference," Daily Labor Report, DLR No. 214, November 5, 1974.

3. The CEA views were set forth most fully in testimony before the U.S. Senate Subcommittee on Manpower and Employment on October 28, 1963. A somewhat revised version of the testimony was reprinted in Economic Report of the President (January 1964), pp. 165-190.

4. Walter W. Heller, New Dimensions of Political Economy (Cambridge, Mass.: Harvard University Press, 1966), p. 8 (footnotes to quotation omitted).

5. Report of the National Commission on Technology, Automation, and Economic Progress, Technology and the American Economy, vol. 1 (Washington, D.C.: U.S. Government Printing Office, 1966), p. 23.

6. See the testimony cited in note 3.

7. The keynote address of Leonard Woodcock to the Conference on Full Employment in New York City on June 14, 1974 (mimeographed), illustrates the point. While his paper effectively made many valid points, his discussion of the "structural" viewpoint attributes it solely to "conservatives," which is quite wrong, and he also portrays this viewpoint as opposed to increasing aggregate demand in the early 1960s, which is even more erroneous.

8. My own views were presented to the U.S. Senate Subcommittee on Manpower and Employment in 1963. Hearings . . ., 88th Cong., 1st sess., pt. 5, pp. 1461-1483. See also "Unemployment and the Tax Cut," ibid., pp. 1787-1794; and "Structural Unemployment in the United States," in Employment Problems of Automation and Advanced Technology, Jack Stieber, ed. (New York: St. Martin's Press, 1966), pp. 128-156.

9. Technology and the American Economy, p. 15. Despite the achievement of the 4.0 percent unemployment rate, the report asserted, "We believe that the potential for general expansion of demand and employment has not yet been exhausted" (p. 34). The report also recommended a number of human-power programs, but with an indefinite and contingent statement concerning when "major attention" should be given to such programs (p. 35).

10. Newsweek, July 14, 1969, p. 79. Lest silence be taken to imply acceptance, I feel obliged to state that this comment indicates that Professor Samuelson misunderstood my position.

11. James Tobin, The New Economics One Decade Older (Princeton: Princeton University Press, 1974), p. 16.

12. Lester C. Thurow, "Redistributional Aspects of Manpower Training Programs," in Lloyd Ulman, ed., Manpower Programs in the Policy Mix (Baltimore: Johns Hopkins University Press, 1973), pp. 83-101 at 84.

13. Further examples are quoted in my article, "Full Employment and the New Economics," Scottish Journal of Political Economy, February 1969, p. 11.

14. See particularly my statement to the U.S. Senate Subcommittee on Manpower, Employment and Poverty on March 25, 1970, Hearings . . ., 91st Cong., 2d sess., pp. 1229-1267; and my statement to the Joint Economic Committee, U.S. Congress, on August 6, 1971, Hearings . . ., 92d Cong., 1st sess., pp. 187-194.

15. The definition change was never publicly announced. However, a speaker for the Bureau of Labor Statistics confirmed that the change had been made and agreed with my estimate of the effect on the unemployment rate at the Joint Economic Committee hearing cited in note 14.

16. Employment and Earnings and Monthly Report on the Labor Force, February 1967.

17. Geoffrey H. Moore, How Full Is Full Employment? (Washington, D.C.: American Enterprise Institute, 1973), p. 14.

18. The figures on participation rates are found in the annual reports of the Bureau of Labor Statistics (initially in Monthly Labor Review, later in Special Labor Force Reports) on educational attainment.

19. Sources of the data substantiating this statement are found in my article, "Fact and Fallacy in Labour Market Analysis," Scottish Journal of Political Economy, February 1970, pp. 95-107 at 105.

20. New York Times, March 13, 1970.

21. My Senate testimony is cited in note 14 above. The House testimony was presented to the Select Subcommittee on Labor in Detroit on March 30, 1970. Hearings . . ., 91st Cong., 2d sess., pp. 603-630.

22. Since I attribute to Stein many of the views that had been elaborated by the new economics in the 1960s, I should note that Walter Heller and Gardner Ackley (both leading proponents of the new economics in its happier days) joined with others in supporting the public service employment program which President Nixon vetoed in 1970.

23. New York Times, January 7, 1971.

24. Unlike some other critics of full employment budgeting, I do not advocate some higher figure for "full employment unemployment." I believe that an appropriate combination of fiscal and human-power policies could be designed which would achieve an unemployment rate well below 4 percent.

CHAPTER

4

THE INFLATION-
UNEMPLOYMENT TRADE-OFF
AND FULL ECONOMIC
RECOVERY
Emile Benoit

It used to be said that a parrot could learn economics if you
could just teach him to say "supply" and "demand." Today it might
with equal justice be claimed that you could teach a parrot the principles of modern economic policy if you could just get him to repeat
endlessly the term: "Phillips Curve." The Phillips Curve shows a
statistically negative relationship between the rate of unemployment
and the rate of inflation: when the unemployment rate is high the rate
of inflation tends to be low, and vice versa. Upon this rock have modern policy makers built their church. Disagreements are mainly over
at what point the tradeoff should be made.
    Some, who are more concerned with the vast waste and human
misery of heavy unemployment—and its political risks—are willing
to accept more inflation. Others, including President Ford and his
chief economic advisors, who are more concerned about the dangers
of further stoking the fires of inflation, are willing to put up with 7
percent unemployment, or more, for years, if necessary, if this will
help moderate inflation. But none of them doubt this dismal tradeoff
is inescapable. One is reminded of the original "dismal science"
economics of Ricardo and Malthus, with its wages fund doctrine which
"proved" that the wages of common labor could never rise above a
bare subsistence level—so that any attempt to improve the conditions
of the masses was hopeless.
    I would like to challenge this commonly held view. To be sure
the Phillips Curve does have some statistical basis, and charts a
genuine (though by no means close) relationship of varying intensity
which has been observed in certain countries in a certain historical

Originally published in The American Journal of Economics
and Sociology 34, no. 4 (October 1975), pp. 337-344.

period. Nevertheless the statistical basis is somewhat weak to carry
such an immense policy load. We are not sure within what range of
variation it will remain true, nor for how long. Furthermore it simply
charts a relationship; it doesn't really explain it. And some of the institutional forces that may have been responsible for temporarily
creating that relationship may now be breaking down. For example,
as strikebreaking becomes institutionally less and less feasible, and
as trade unions become more and more strongly organized with more
and more political power, then they become less and less deterred
from striking to achieve wage increases even in periods of heavy unemployment.

I

One initial observation is that ever since 1950 the U.S. cost of
living has risen every single year,[1] even in periods of recession, and
when raw material costs have declined. Thus recession and unemployment can no longer stop inflation, but, at most only slow it down.
A second observation is that recently new forces appear to be at work
to give an explosive quality to inflation: in the last year and a half inflation has been at unparalleled rates despite unemployment rates ex-
ceeding anything seen since the great depression.

Obviously the Phillips Curve tells only a part of the complex
truth about the relationship between unemployment and inflation. To
achieve true prosperity we will have to give equal recognition to the
rest of the story, which has so far been largely ignored.

The simplistic Phillips-Curve approach makes it appear that
the only possible way to stop inflation is to create a lot of slack in
the economy by means of tight money and cuts in government spending. Thus interest rates have been raised sharply, and the money
supply, corrected for price increases, was cut by a tenth. And—
though this is not generally realized—real federal expenditures on
goods and services, i.e., outlays corrected for price increases, have
been cut by 28 percent between 1968 and 1974. And now for the first
time since World War II even the expenditure of state and local governments are beginning to decline in real terms. This did succeed
in creating a slack, all right: production was off by a tenth, and the
unemployment rate rose by a seventh. Yet prices kept rising. The
existence of major recession and violent inflation at the same time
points to a basic weakness in the whole theory.

These deflationary policies seek to cut the total of spending,
with the classical notion that if inflation is too many dollars chasing
too few goods, then if you reduce the number of dollars chasing the

goods you are bound to moderate the inflation. What isn't recognized is that if goods are produced only in order to be sold, then if you cut back the size of the markets you are likely at the same time to cut back the amount of goods produced and offered for sale. In which case the gap between the amount of goods available and the number of dollars chasing them may be little if any narrowed, and inflation may by no means have been ended. By this route it may take a very long time, indeed, to eliminate the excess of dollars over goods, and it's an extremely painful and dangerous way to do it, in terms of lost production and lives wasted and embittered by unnecessary unemployment.

II

What I should like now to suggest is the novel theory that a more effective way to end inflation (and to produce full economic recovery at the same time) is to produce not less but more—sufficiently more so that supply overtakes demand, and begins to drive prices down—while making sure by way of controls and taxation that after-tax income and demand do not rise too quickly, especially for items not essential for the national welfare.

How could this be done? Hitherto we have thought solely in terms of achieving the right level of aggregate demand, and we assumed that this by itself would assure the achievement of full employment. If for Phillips-Curve reasons we felt we had to sacrifice full employment, we believed that it would at least give us a tolerable level of unemployment plus price stability. What we now are beginning to realize is that even if we could agree on the "right" level of aggregate demand, and could arrange our policies so that it was attained and maintained, this would still meet only half the problem. The other half is the question of the elasticity of supply—how supply reacts to changes in aggregate demand. This is something we can no longer assume will take care of itself.

In fact in highly concentrated industries (where the bulk of the product is produced by a small number of producers), there is a persistent tendency to respond to demand increases by raising prices instead of increasing output at the previously existing prices. And when demand slumps, production costs rise, because of suboptimal utilization of fixed-cost production facilities, and institutional difficulties in making any comparable offsetting savings on wages.

With higher costs, producers feel they must quote higher prices, to conserve their margins and enable them to finance increasingly expensive plant replacements. They can usually get the higher prices, or at least maintain high prices, despite stagnant or shrinking demand, by the use of their market power: the relatively few producers responsible for a large share of the market recognize that price cuts leading to retaliatory price wars would ultimately benefit none of the contenders and might paradoxically even get them into trouble with the Antitrust Division of the Justice Department as evidence of destructive competition with an intent to monopolize. Therefore they tacitly agree to keep prices stable, or even to increase them to reflect higher costs—plus a little extra.

Thus in good times and bad there is a continued tendency for prices to rise. Moreover the strongly organized trade unions which are particularly powerful in the concentrated industries are regularly given wage increases far in excess of their increases in productivity, resulting in further cost increases that are passed on to the public in the form of higher prices.

There are two main arguments against this whole point of view. First it is said that once the interested parties have achieved their optimum oligopoly price they have no incentive for further price increases. Hence this factor would not explain continuously rising prices. This argument ignores the gradualness with which market power is acquired and strengthened, and the tentative and slow way in which it is learned how to use it effectively, and to circumvent the obstacles established by antitrust.

It is not even clear that the optimum oligopoly price is determinate. If it is, it is certainly not easy to recognize. It is not surprising that it should be approached via the respectable technique of successive approximations. Also, it keeps being pushed up by rising labor costs.

The second argument is that statistical studies show no positive correlation between the degree of concentration and the extent of price increases. Indeed, industries where four companies control more than half the industry's output show lower price increases than industries where four companies control less than half of the industry's output.[2] This is a serious argument, but it does not rigorously demonstrate that market power may not be a factor in inflation. For the large companies in highly concentrated industry may make sufficient productivity gains so that they could provide moderate wage increases and maintain profits even with price cuts. If instead they provide high wage increases, and medium price increases, they set an influential example for other less productive companies. The smaller companies in less concentrated industries may have quite sufficient market power to exact sizable price increases, and in their cases they must, first of all, pay the higher prices for their industrial inputs to be bought from the concentrated industries, and second they must pay more or less the same wage increases as already announced in the concentrated industries, even though productivity gains may be minimal. In that case, prices may have to be raised even more than in the concentrated industries to achieve any profits at all. Thus the fact that their prices may rise slightly more than in the highly concentrated industries does not really prove that market power is not an important transmission belt for inflation.

A true prosperity policy would therefore attempt more than to achieve the right level of demand. It would pay equal attention to assure that supply was freely and adequately responsive to demand. Obviously this is no easy task. The general principle involved is that no wage increases should be permitted in unionized industries in excess of productivity increases, and no price increases permitted in concentrated industries in excess of demonstrable increases in costs. (Perhaps such excessive increases might not be barred in advance, but retroactively nullified by a 100 percent tax on such excessive wage increases and no profits derived from such price increases.) Trade unions could still win real wage increases but only by helping to bring about productivity increases, which made it possible to produce more with the same number of workers. Companies could still increase their after-tax profits, but only by increasing their production and sales, or cutting costs—not by raising prices.

III

Obviously it is a lot easier to propound such a general policy than it would be to specify its detailed mode of operation and enforcement. And if (as is likely) this would require more regulatory agencies, there are obvious dangers that they might be "captured" by the industries they were intended to regulate, as have so many other regulatory commissions. The difficulties are obvious. Clearly substantial governmental reforms would be required to curtail corruption and influence peddling, and to assure that the additional governmental powers would be properly used. But if this is what it takes to eliminate inflationary recession (as I believe to be the case), then it is worth it. Our government takes incredible pains over such matters as social security, labor organizations, restraints on agricultural production, security regulation, etc., all of which are worth doing but none of which are remotely as important as the elimination of inflationary recessions.

There is a complication that must at least be mentioned. It now appears that a new long range force making for inflation has entered the picture, namely shortages emanating from depletion of low cost and readily available energy and other resources, plus rising costs of pollution-avoidance and pollution-control. I have discussed these problems and their long term solutions in a recent University of California public lecture entitled "The Political Economy of Shortages" and in a piece called "Must Growth Stop?" in the Kenneth Boulding Festschrift.[3] These matters involve essentially long term issues, but on one point they also have important implications for short range policy. If in any case for many years we are now going to be under severe inflationary pressures arising from built-in depletion and environmental factors, then it is cruel and senseless to keep a large part of our labor force unnecessarily unemployed as well—both wasting their potential production, and foolishly provoking dangerous revolutionary tensions.

It would be far safer, as well as more humane, we have argued, to reduce the tension between supply and demand by expanding production and employment while—by way of controls and taxes—restraining the amount of additional purchasing power generated by the additional production.

But there is one further complication which none of the recovery programs, liberal or conservative, seem to have taken into account. Just to get full employment, it is not good enough simply to restore previous patterns of employment and production.

From this point of view, it may be a mistake to depend primarily on tax cuts to promote recovery as we are now doing. For thirty years I have argued for deficit-financed tax cuts as a prime means of recovery from recession.[4] So I must be granted a certain sympathy for the device. But the difficulty with tax cuts is that they tend to restore whatever it was that we were previously doing. If we have to eliminate or attenuate certain of these things, in order to meet the long term problems looming up ahead, then restoring these things is an inefficient way of ending the recession. Even if it works, it will only accentuate the problems we will face immediately after the recession is ended. What we need then are not tax cuts, to restore past patterns of production and employment, but selective subsidies and government contracts to stimulate production and employment in the industries that we will need to encourage for national survival.

One industry that needs saving is our railroad network, which under the onslaught of the politically powerful highway lobby is being allowed to fall to pieces. This despite the fact that at any moment our oil imports might be discontinued and part of our oil supply diverted to support our allies. Railroad transportation is in any case vastly more economical and less polluting. An example of a new industry that should be quickly expanded is the production of methanol, or wood-alcohol, which can be made of garbage and other organic wastes. A mixture of gasoline and up to 15 percent of methanol will run in ordinary gasoline engines with cooler engines, less pollution, and only slight sacrifice of mileage—and at a substantial economy as well.

These are merely two random samples on which we could start spending a good deal of money rather quickly with excellent results. Also we should quickly start intensive research and development on wind generators and other indirect or direct forms of solar power since solar energy is the only type of power that does not raise the temperature of the earth and will not make it unlivable in a couple of centuries of continuing growth in power utilization.

IV

Those who worry that we can't afford to spend federal funds on such projects should remember that federal expenditure on goods and services is already down by 28 percent from 1968 levels, in real terms which, at today's prices is equal to $45 billion. If we could now start spending $45 billion a year on the solutions to our environmental problems the recession would be over almost immediately. And with the reduced need for unemployment compensation and other transfer payments on the one hand, and greatly increased tax revenues on the other, fiscal problems would be eased.

Inflationary problems, though, would be accentuated unless measures were adopted like those earlier recommended to restrict the income and price increases generated by the expansion of output. And special measures would be needed to restrict our increased imports of items we could not truly afford.

But these inconveniences appear minor if we could thereby fully recover our economic health and vigor as well as safeguard our future (and the future of our children) on this planet. It is our view that these goals are not only compatible but positively interrelated. We must, once and for all, abandon laissez-faire and recognize that government, though ill equipped to run particular industries, is essential for mobilizing a national consensus on priorities, and for establishing a network of incentives that will assure its implementation. It now begins to appear that this is almost as important in solving our short term, as our long term problems.

NOTES

1. Revised estimates do show a 0.4 percent decline in consumer prices in 1955, but the more comprehensive price index of the Implicit Deflator for the GNP shows a 1.3 percent increase.

2. See Steven Lastgarten, Industrial Concentration and Inflation (Washington, D.C.: American Institute for Public Policy Research, 1975).

3. The main substance of these two pieces is to be published in a series of three articles in The Bulletin of the Atomic Scientists, starting in December or January, entitled "The Coming Era of Shortages," "Intertemporal Justice: Saving Future Generations" and "First Steps to Human Survival."

4. See, e.g., my debate with former Senator Paul Douglas, "Tax Cuts Now?" in the New Republic, August 13, 1962.

5

TOWARD EQUALITY THROUGH
FULL EMPLOYMENT
Robert Lekachman

Full employment did not cause the Great Inflation of 1974 and 1975. During 1974 unemployment averaged a shade under 5 percent, enough to alarm Europeans and Japanese and lose elections for French and German politicians.

Nor did greedy labor unions start inflation. With the exception of a few fat construction contracts, wage agreements have been lagging far behind the cost of living. If they kept their jobs, average blue- and white-collar workers lost eight percent of their purchasing power in the last two years. In fact the average factory worker was worse off in 1975 than he was in 1966. In 1967 dollars, he got $115.58 nine years ago. This year he got only $114.38.

Big government deficits aren't responsible for this inflation. The deficits got bigger and bigger because the Internal Revenue Service was collecting less money from the taxpayers. Tax receipts shrank because people lost jobs, small businessmen went broke, and large corporations cut their payrolls instead of their prices.

THE REAL CAUSES OF INFLATION

Inflation was stimulated by:
(1) The pricing policies of the OPEC cartel which acted on gasoline, home heating oil, synthetic fabrics, and chemical fertilizers;

Originally published in Social Policy 5, no. 3 (September/ October 1974), pp. 6-11. © 1974 by Social Policy Corporation.

(2) A worldwide increase in demand for American farm products which enriched farmers and food processors at the expense of American city dwellers;

(3) The decision way back in 1972 by Dr. Arthur F. Burns and his Federal Reserve Board colleagues to pump money and credit into the economy in order to help reelect Richard Nixon;

(4) Two devaluations of the American dollar. After devaluation foreigners bought our food, raw materials, and finished goods at prices lower in terms of their own money than they had been. When their business boomed, American exporters raised their prices for the home folks. Devaluation also made German and Japanese cars, cameras, TV sets, and electronic gadgets more expensive. Yen and marks traded for fewer American dollars than before devaluation.

(5) The behavior of our own monopolists and oligopolists. General Motors and its chums added $1000 to the price of an average car between 1974 and 1975 even though the customers were deciding to drive their old heaps another year or turning to thriftier Toyotas, Datsuns, Renaults, and Volkswagons. Food processors and energy companies ripped off huge profits from shortages which they often helped to create.

PRICES AND JOBS

In 1973, 1974, and 1975 we had lots of unemployment and lots of inflation. In sharp contrast, we enjoyed both decreasing unemployment and nearly steady prices between 1961 and the middle of 1965. The cost of living each year rose only 1.5 percent. Gross National Product on the average increased over 5 percent each year and unemployment steadily dropped from the 6.7 percent which greeted John Kennedy in January 1961.

Something like full employment and price stability were experienced during World War II and again during the Korean War. During 1944 and 1945 unemployment fell below 1 percent.

When President Ford, Alan Greenspan, William Simon, and Arthur Burns warn Congress not to spend money on public jobs, mass transportation, new homes, better education and health care, and improved benefits to the poor and unemployed, because more spending will reawaken the inflationary dragon, what these Four Horsemen of economic despair are really saying is this: Given half a chance, their big business friends will raise their prices and profits so much that unions in a desperate attempt to keep up will insist on the sort of large wage improvements which will serve as an excuse for a new round of price hikes.

The Republicans are also claiming that the United States can't afford full employment. Conservatives and reactionaries who advocate 7 or 8 percent unemployment for the next three years and promise (promise?) 6 percent unemployment by 1979 are telling high school and university graduates to wait around for two or three or four years. Perhaps if they haven't forgotten everything they learned, there will be some sort of job for them. The partisans of unemployment are advising women, blacks, and Hispanics to accept without complaint the loss of jobs that the civil rights statutes of the 1960s and the affirmative action plans based on them got them a year or two ago.

Last January when General Motors shut down one shift in its Linden, New Jersey plant, it fired all of its women employees. As the accountants say, "Last in, first out."

What we really can't afford is unemployment. Each extra 1 percent of unemployment costs 900,000 jobs, $50 billion of unproduced Gross National Product, and $14 billion in uncollected taxes. Conservatives who hate big deficits should be screaming for full employment. This is the financial bill. The human costs include destroyed hopes and dreams, reduced standards of living, and high rates of crime, drug abuse, and alcoholism.

The United States can have full employment.

We know how to lick inflation.

Inflation is the consequence of monetary validations of more claims upon the Gross National Product than there is output, at current prices, to be distributed. On the evidence of recent experience, moderate inflation when accompanied by steady real growth and comparatively stable income distribution by size and function appears to be tolerable to people in quite varied economic circumstances. In the United States, however, a flaw in this tacit social contract has been an inability to deliver a fair approximation of full employment save under exceptional circumstances, usually during a major war.

What I shall maintain here is this: the prerequisites of full employment combined with price stability relate to equity of sacrifice and equity of reward. These prerequisites are immediately four in number and in the longer run there is probably a fifth as well. They are:

1. A guarantee by federal, state, and local governments of public employment as a reliable alternative to private jobs in both good and bad economic times.
2. For those unable or unwilling to work (in all probability a very small number) income maintenance at a decent level as a matter of right.

3. An incomes policy, focused upon large corporations, professional societies, and unions, as powerful and permanent as the organizations which necessitate this public response.
4. On grounds of equity and price stability alike, a serious policy of redistributive taxation.
5. In the future a gradually increasing public and diminishing private sphere of activity, a realization of the Keynesian vision of a "somewhat comprehensive socialization of investment."[1]

I turn accordingly to a brief discussion of the desirability of these alterations in the American way of life.

PUBLIC JOBS

Current, well-intentioned congressional job creation proposals with one outstanding exception (of which more shortly) treat the problem which they address as temporary. Thus S. 2993, introduced on February 8, 1974 by Senator Jacob Javits and several colleagues, links itself to the energy crisis, establishes "a special program of emergency energy employment," relates outlays to an unemployment trigger of 6 percent, and speaks throughout of "transitional public service employment opportunities."

"Transitional" positions are likely to be second-class jobs evaluated suspiciously by civil service associations and unions of public employees as potential infringements upon benefit, job security, and wage standards won over many years by painful negotiation. The new jobs are exceedingly likely to be attacked as leaf-raking or hole-filling activities to be eliminated just as soon as possible. Public preferences for private over public activity are almost certain to be reinforced by this approach to the alleviation of private sector unemployment.

A far superior design is embodied in H.R. 15476, introduced on June 19, 1974 by Congressmen Augustus Hawkins of California and Henry Reuss of Wisconsin, and in August of the same year by Hubert Humphrey in the Senate. Their proposal, a revival and extension of the 1945 Wagner-Murray Full Employment Bill (which in emasculated form survived as the Employment Act of 1946), aims "to establish a national policy and nationwide machinery for guaranteeing to all adult Americans able and willing to work the availability of equal opportunities for useful and rewarding employment." The measure's short title identifies both objectives and the time required to approach them: "This Act may be cited as the Equal Opportunity and Full Employment Act of 1976."

Unlike S. 2993 and similar measures, the bill is designed as a permanent obligation of Congress and the president. It imposes upon the president the annual requirement, updated at six-month intervals, to formulate a full employment and production program. It issues an instruction to the chief executive to convert the existing Manpower Reports into detailed examinations of the labor force and careful surveys of public employment opportunities. The United States Employment Service, encouragingly retitled the United States Full Employment Service, will henceforth harbor as a new instrument a Job Guarantee Office charged with supplying "useful and rewarding employment for any American, able and willing to work but not yet working, unable otherwise to obtain work and applying to such office for assistance." Officials of the office will be empowered to contract with private and voluntary agencies as well as local planning councils. As a humane society should, the bill adopts an expanded definition of employability: any job seeker "who presents himself or herself in person at the Full Employment Office . . . shall be considered prima facie 'willing and able' to work." Job hunters are registered in a Standby Job Corps "available for public service work upon projects and activities that are approved as a part of community public service work reservoirs established by community boards." Corps members will be paid at rates related to their employment at a "suitable and comparable job," but in no case below legal minima.

As a serious and sophisticated attempt to grapple with the concrete details involved in the implementation of comprehensive job guarantees, this proposal is notable for its emphasis upon social and economic equity, and the quality of life for citizens in all social stations. As the recent deterioration in the ratio of black to white income reminds us, high unemployment is mildly egalitarian in its effects and sluggish labor markets are invariably hostile to the claims of disadvantaged groups which are latecomers to the American celebration.

As an anti-inflationary policy, an additional equity consideration obtrudes itself. As intelligent conservatives like Dr. Arthur F. Burns realize, monetary and fiscal restraints always increase general unemployment by imposing disproportionately severe burdens upon the most vulnerable elements of the labor force—the black, young, and female. Dr. Burns, a wistful believer in free markets, nevertheless endorsed Senator Javits's $4 billion public job measure because he recognized that the sort of restrictive monetary and fiscal policy which he favored is politically facilitated by the sort of job creation measures which mitigate the inequities of tight money and federal budget surpluses.

Flat job guarantees promise additional benefits. Public sector expansion is energy and resource thrifty, particularly if the new jobs are located in health care, education, security of persons and property, environmental conservation, and fire protection. Full employment would surely stimulate job redesign, flexible work scheduling, study and recreational sabbaticals, and a greatly to be desired general humanization of work in offices and factories. By no means least important, full employment promotes social cohesion and the integration into the labor force of that under- and unemployed underclass whose existence Gunnar Myrdal postulates as a mark of an underdeveloped society.

INCOME MAINTENANCE

In our country, income maintenance programs include old age and survivors' benefits, veterans' pensions, Aid to the Families of Dependent Children, food stamps, and a variety of other measures, including, I suppose, subsidies to Pan Am, the Penn Central, Lockheed, and other needy corporate citizens. Eligibility is premised upon appropriate status: honorable as in the instance of veterans and the elderly, dishonorable as in the notorious case of the welfare population. Neither legislatures nor courts have defined as a general right an entitlement to public aid. Intermittently courts have moved tentatively in the direction of providing due process protections to welfare beneficiaries. Most recently, the Nixon Supreme Court has retreated toward an older conception of welfare as gift or gratuity rather than consequence of membership in civilized society.[2]

Some persons even on liberal employability criteria cannot work. Others, either because they prefer the care of young children or alternative life-styles, prefer not to work. The numbers in both categories, in all likelihood, are a small percentage of the labor force. Unwilling workers are unlikely to be productive employees. Hence on both efficiency and equity grounds, the argument is compelling for substituting a general measure of income maintenance for existing cash grant programs covering separate groups. The most convenient mechanism is some version of a negative income tax (NIT), preferably one which is explicitly redistributive in its impact. As a device, an NIT is defined by the presence of a basic grant and tax upon earnings which at some breaking point reduces the grant to zero and enrolls the grant recipient into the company of ordinary taxpayers. Thus, even at 1974 prices, a $1,000 per person basic grant in tandem with a 50 percent tax on earnings would define as potential beneficiaries not only unemployed persons but also substantial numbers of fully employed but moderately remunerated individuals. Until a man or woman reached an income of $12,000[3] as head of a family of four, he or she would gain either in outright cash subventions (at the low end of the income scale) or tax reductions (at the upper end).

The numbers with which one tags both basic grants and taxes upon earnings relates to the degree of income redistribution which is desired and the quantity of essential health, counseling, educational, and psychiatric services which is available at zero or low cost. Thus, if in the near future Congress enacted a universal health-care measure which approximated the original Kennedy-Griffiths bill, liberalized food stamps, expanded the supply and lowered the rentals of public housing, and multiplied the quantity of convenient, low-cost mass transportation, even egalitarians (like myself) would favor lower basic grants and, possibly, higher compensating taxes upon earnings than they would in the absence of some or all of these social necessities or amenities.

The most persuasive of all arguments for an NIT is its association with individual dignity. As currently administered, welfare degrades both those who administer it and those who ostensibly benefit from it. Once welfare is translated into universal income guarantees, it is possible to substitute the neutral, universally and equally detested bureaucracy of the Internal Revenue Service for the disdained, special-interest welfare officials. Possibly the greatest of psychic benefits a humane society confers upon its inhabitants is a secure confidence in personal worth. Such a sense makes life tolerable for those blessed by it. From society's standpoint, decent self-regard encourages the character of individual effort which eventuates in training, active job search, and subsequent productive contribution.

I find it difficult to escape the conclusion that malevolence, contempt for the poor, low regard for ''losers,'' and willingness to blame victims (to borrow William Ryan's expressive language) are all implicated in the public's reluctance to move from a welfare system universally excoriated (not least by its ''beneficiaries'') to a simpler, more dignified, and, in the long run, less expensive alternative. Nixon's Family Assistance Plan (FAP) failed partly because Mr. Nixon ultimately sabotaged his own proposal, partly because critics on the left resisted its malign combination of meager benefits and covert violations of civil liberties,[4] but largely because, despite quantities of soggy administration rhetoric in praise of workfare and payrolls instead of welfare and welfare rolls, conservatives persisted in resisting FAP as a give-away, a gift of the taxpayers' hard-earned dollars to morally unworthy men and women, many of them with the poor taste to be black, unmarried, or both.

CONTROLS

Among economists, traditional dislike of price and wage controls is allied to a strong preference for free markets. On the one
hand, these markets register the shifting tastes and preferences of
the customers, and, on the other, the responses of sellers to these
tastes within the constraints imposed by the necessity to hire labor,
rent space, buy raw materials, and borrow money. The charms of the
free market are several, but above all two: it operates by itself; and
all the actors, to recall Alfred Marshall's comment, are motivated
not by altruism, a weak impulse, but by self-interest, an exceedingly
well-developed one. Dense consumers are often astounded by their
dissatisfaction with their purchases. If capable of learning from experience, they gradually of their own accord improve the quality of
their selections. Stupid business people who misjudge their market
and spend their scarce cash on inappropriate combinations of the factors of production go broke in short order. The resources which they
mishandled pass into the control of more efficient rivals. Tough for
the losers. Splendid for the economy as a whole.

Like other branches of theology, free-market economics is an
idealized version of human arrangements. The case for permanent
controls is associated with a shortage of free markets, the affection
of most Americans for size in corporations as well as defensive line-
men, and the consequent reluctance of presidents and congresspeople
to apply antitrust statutes effectively to the giant corporations which
dominate the American economy. In their respective industries, the
four largest corporations control 99 percent of autos, 96 percent of
aluminum, 80 percent of cigarettes, 72 percent of soaps and deter-
gents, and so on.[5]

Market power confers upon those who possess it the discretion
to choose, within varying but usually wide limits, combinations of high
prices and reduced sales or alternative packages of low prices and
larger sales. The resources of oligopolists are large enough to facilitate expenditures on advertising and marketing which manipulate
rather than respond to the market. Again the freedom is, fortunately,
less than absolute, as such spectacular disasters as the Edsel indicate. It is, nevertheless, considerable enough to render a fantasy the
economist's vision of consumers rationally choosing the items which
maximize their satisfaction. In general, market leaders opt for an
inflationary strategy, a combination of high prices and heavy advertising. So, no doubt, would you and I behave, if we were lucky enough
to be oligopolists.

Economists cling to their affections for free markets, partly
out of loyalty to their own training and partly because free-market

theory is such a beautifully articulated intellectual structure. When textbook discussion turns, usually quite briefly, to monopoly and oligopoly, authors sadly agree that, yes, these departures from competition raise prices, reduce output, and waste resources on advertising. What can they do? As Edwin Mansfield glumly reveals in an excellent new introductory volume, <u>Economics: Principles, Problems, Decisions</u> (Norton, 1974), "There is no single unified model of oligopoly behavior." Aside from outright collusion, the theoretical explanations are a choice between Paul Sweezy's 1939 "jeu d' esprit," the kinked demand curve, and Von Neumann's and Morgenstern's 1944 exercise in the theory of games.

I believe, to depart from the common wisdom on this point, that bad theory is worse than no theory at all. Which suggests that the appropriate reactions to inflation require, as heavy supplements to received economics, common observation and the application of enlightened ethical principle. As all know, the causes of inflation are multiple: policy blunders, the politics of Vietnam escalation and the manipulations of CREEP, detente as a re-election ploy, bad luck, bad weather, mutinous anchovies, pricerigging by the Organization of Petroleum Exporting Countries, and simultaneous business cycle peaks in the leading trading nations. One ought not exaggerage the efficacy of even wholesome remedies. Wage and price controls will not improve the behavior of Arab oil producers nor alleviate shortages of food and fertilizer. Wage and price controls do appropriately react to that element of inflation which derives from the exercise of concentrated market power. Since in the absence of unanticipated alterations in the American economy, large economic units will continue to dominate the scene and their managers will continue, without effective public supervision, to engage in private planning, the appropriate response is to make public supervision effective.

For the real public policy choice is not between planning and competition, it is between private planning regulated by the self-interest of autonomous corporate managers and private planning supervised by elected officials and their agents. Wage and price controls, land use standards, environmental and occupational safety regulations, even rationing and allocation, are not distortions of competitive markets for the adequate reason that such markets are of diminishing consequence. Indeed, a rational set of controls and regulations represents an opportunity to correct the distortions imposed upon the use of resources by the operations of concentrated private economic power.

In the American and other advanced economies, cost-push inflation is always either evident or incipient. In the last two or three years American unions have behaved with unusual restraint, partly, one guesses, because of an unsympathetic national administration.

Nevertheless, the temptation is strong, particularly when prices out-
pace wages, for unions to seek improvements in excess of productivity
gains and for their employers to grant them in the expectation of passing them on to the unorganized customers.

As the recent performance of economists demonstrates anew,
prophecy is hazardous. All the same, I venture the guess that in the
next year wage-price controls will either reappear (despite President
Ford's promise to avoid them) in the context of other anti-inflationary
measures or, a revival of the policies of 1969 and 1970, Nixonomics
Mark I, will plunge the economy into a deep depression—a nightmare
which the pollsters assert a growing majority of Americans now anticipate.

The minimal characteristics of effective controls feature per-
manence and equity. From mid-1971 to the end of 1972, Phase 1 and
Phase 2 controls restrained wages more effectively than property income. Reluctantly unions went along with a modest wage guidepost.
In the longer run, however, no controls perceived as unfair by an important economic group will long endure. Equity of course is an evolving concept and one of the benefits of establishing wage-price control
as a permanent government function is the development of an informal
case of control and the refinement of standards based upon experience.

Controls liberate monetary and fiscal policy, but they are not of
course a substitute for such policy. During severe inflation, effective
controls facilitate monetary policy by limiting the corporate borrowing
required to finance inventories at rising prices. By diverting demand
to controlled industries,[6] they diminish demand in the competitive
sector and simplify the tasks of fiscal policy.

Very much as public job creation is an essential response to
the unemployment caused by anti-inflationary efforts, controls are
the necessary corollary of fiscal and monetary responses to excess
demand and cost push. Here I leave open both the extent and variety
of controls. Congress will be well-advised to grant the controllers
considerable discretion in how they respond to various types of inflation and various combinations of inflation and recessions.

Controls ought to be as pervasive as the departures from the
economist's ideal of free competition. One should ask no more. It
is dangerous to seek less.

TAXES

Since 1961 presidents and congresses have conspired to reduce
taxes five times—thrice across the board in 1964, 1969, and 1971, and
twice selectively in 1961 and 1965. As a consequence, between 1955

and 1970, corporate income taxes as a percentage of federal collections dropped from 20 to 12 percent. During the same 15 years, payroll taxes nearly doubled, rising from 8 to 15 percent. Corporate taxes, falling partly on stockholders, are progressive. Payroll taxes are notoriously regressive. According to Brookings studies, the Treasury would now be $16 billion richer each year if the 1969 and 1971 slashes in personal and corporate income taxes had not been enacted. A shrinking tax base limits funds potentially available for income maintenance, housing, health, humanpower training, and community development, a point thoroughly appreciated by such conservative economists as Milton Friedman and apparently less well-recognized by liberal economists who continue to advocate tax reduction as all-purpose economic therapy.

It follows that during a 1974-style inflation, sharp tax increases are potentially equitable as well as anti-inflationary if they are imposed entirely upon large inheritances and gifts, corporate profits, large private incomes, and the tax shelters which currently protect the unneedy. The $20-25 billion which such taxes might raise ought in the interest of rude justice finance new public jobs, facilitate reductions of payroll levies upon the first portions of earnings, and finance income maintenance. If $10 billion was devoted to public jobs, an equal amount to tax reliefs for low- and moderate-income individuals and families, there would still be $5 billion remaining as a reduction of excess demand.

Because some such package would be and would appear fair, it could serve as a part of an implicit social contract with unions to moderate contract demands. As tax benefits were made available, real take-home pay would rise. Possibly just as important, rank and file outrage at soaring profits and shrinking real wages would be alleviated.

SOCIALIZATION OF INVESTMENT: A LONG-RUN PROSPECT

My combination of public job creation, income maintenance, limitations upon property as well as labor income, and redistributive taxation is certainly open to the criticism that it promotes consumption and discourages innovation and investment. As a conventional argument might go, higher corporate taxes and higher taxes on large incomes discourage the taking of entrepreneurial risks on new products and processes, and dampen the incentives of corporate executives to clamber up the corporate ladder. Persons may shorten their working week, lengthen their holidays and weekends, and transfer their capital to Swiss or Belgian banks.

One needn't swallow whole such self-serving complaints. Sweden, a country whose standard of living by some measures equals the American, has for nearly half a century been administered by social democrats who have pursued far more egalitarian tax, social service, and humanpower policies than the United States. What probably counts more than after-tax income is one's position in the packing order as measured by pre-tax salary and bonus. Is it likely that halving Mr. Geneen's princely compensation of $900,000 or so and adjusting his subordinates' rewards commensurately would cause Mr. Geneen and his associates to sulk and go home with their marbles? For true competitors, corporate-style, it is winning that counts, not the size of the purse.

I could be wrong. Concede, arguendo, that the present scale of rewards to managers and entrepreneurs is essential to the evocation of their present efforts and talents. Private investment would then shrink. In the absence of government response, the well-known multiplier effects of reduced investment would diminish aggregate demand and employment.

I should look upon such effects with equanimity if not positive delight, for the threat of enduring depression would create favorable conditions for the expansion of public investment to fill the gap. If one believes, as I do, that our single greatest national need is an expansion of the communal enterprises which distinguish civilized from uncivilized societies, then the threats of entrepreneurs and rentiers lose their terror.

Although I consider it highly unlikely that another $25 billion extracted from the wealthy and strong will seriously alter the American version of market capitalism, I will happily take the risk. I invite others to join me.

NOTES

1. J. M. Keynes, The General Theory of Employment, Interest and Money (New York: Harcourt, 1936), p. 378.

2. The leading case is Wyman v. James which affirmed the constitutional authority of New York City welfare authorities to condition continued benefits for Mrs. James upon her agreement to accept mandatory home visits by her caseworker. Writing for the majority, Mr. Justice Blackmun asserted, in the course of denying Mrs. James's claim that the Fourth Amendment protected her privacy against invasions by public authority, that "one who dispenses purely private charity naturally has an interest in and expects to

know how his charitable funds are utilized and put to work. The public, when it is the provider, rightly expects the same."

3. As of mid-1974, the income median was approximately $12,700.

4. As Daniel Patrick Moynihan's ex parte account runs, social workers opposed FAP out of fear for their jobs and status and welfare-rights proponents because they feared erosion of their support among welfare beneficiaries. See The Politics of Income Maintenance, Coping, a collection of essays, both published by Random House.

5. Professional societies operate in similar ways to restrict output and raise fees. Minimum fee schedules promulgated by bar associations and mutually beneficial alliances among the AMA, Blue Cross-Blue Shield, and hospitals have turned lawyers and especially doctors into affluent Americans.

6. I assume that, save in rare emergencies, controls will focus upon large corporations and the unions with which they deal, plus the stronger professional societies. These are the loci of market power.

6

**INFLATION AND
UNEMPLOYMENT:
JOBS ABOVE ALL**
Bennett Harrison

Much has been written and publicly debated about the apparent inability of the private sector to generate enough jobs at decent wages to support all those who want to work. Since 1964, federal employment policy has emphasized education and training to increase the "employability" of the underemployed. In an economy replete with obstacles to the free mobility of labor across space and among occupations, given the legitimate desire of many not to have to move, and with too few jobs paying nonpoverty wages, such a policy could of course never be more than supplementary, and a host of evaluations of the Great Society's (and later) "human capital"-oriented humanpower programs have now confirmed this expectation.

Since 1971, we have begun to confront the problem directly through federally funded public service job creation. The magnitude of such programs is expected to grow in the future, as is the role of public investment or selective tax cuts to stimulate underdeveloped or lagging industries (such as the railroads). The Full Employment Act of 1976, introduced in Congress in 1974 by South Los Angeles Rep. Augustus Hawkins, would require the federal government to guarantee a "job at decent pay" to every American wanting to work, or a guaranteed minimum income until a job could be found or created. This— or any other major labor demand-creation program—would require truly massive public investment, government consumption of privately produced goods and services, transfers to state and local governments, strong minimum wage policies, and price-profit-wage controls, perhaps indefinitely.

Originally published in Social Policy 5, no. 6 (March/April 1975), pp. 36-42. © 1975 by Social Policy Corporation.

Many obstacles stand in the way of the serious consideration of such comprehensive economic planning for full employment. Perhaps the most pervasive is the fear that such expansion must necessarily produce intolerable inflation: a general increase in the price level (as distinct from a condition of high relative prices for certain goods and services). Actually, many economists believe that workers (especially the poor) often benefit from inflation and high rates of economic growth, especially in terms of increased bargaining power—provided government does not resort to deliberately engineered recessions (Leonard Rapping's "political business cycles") to "ease the pressure." But it cannot be denied that many workers qua consumers and pensioners are injured by inflation, too, especially when it becomes concentrated in the key areas of food and fuel.

In any case, workers/consumers certainly believe that inflation is invariably harmful to them. Nine percent of the labor force may be currently unemployed, but 100 percent are faced with higher prices for a whole host of consumption goods. And it is to this belief in the inflationary consequences of full employment that those who oppose the latter have directed their propaganda.

I will argue that modern American inflation is sometimes created, and almost always sustained and reinforced, by monopoly (or, more precisely, oligopoly) power at the core of American industry, and by the inability or unwillingness of the American political system at all levels to engage in the kind of basic economic planning that is becoming increasingly necessary in a complex system as a way of anticipating and preventing supply bottlenecks and uncoordinated interactions among the various sectors of the economy.

Inflation should be attacked by addressing the structural factors that exacerbate it. Even in the absence of the political will for such an attack, inflation may not be so terrible that we should be willing to deliberately engineer recessions because of our fear of it.

INFLATION: THE ORTHODOX VIEW

The economy is assumed, at any point in time, to be capable of producing a "potential gross national product": that total output of goods and services which the system could produce (with given technology) if all resources (including labor) were fully utilized. When any resources are unemployed, the "actual GNP" will fall short of this potential.

All popular explanations of how inflation gets triggered begin with the condition of "excess effective demand" ("too much income chasing too few goods," "demand-pull"). This is typically attributed

to liberal public policy: either the federal government runs large deficits,[1] or the Federal Reserve system creates too much money. For
there to be a general excess of demand, leading to a general inflation,
actual GNP would have to be about equal to potential GNP, i.e., there
would have to be something close to full employment of all resources.
Thus, deficit spending (or expansionary monetary policy) to stimulate
the economy when actual GNP falls short of potential GNP might create
excess demand (and therefore a relative price increase) for some
goods and services, but in itself it cannot create general excess demand (and therefore an increase in the general price level—inflation).
The popular belief that government deficit spending or "loose money"
policy always produces inflation is simply incorrect.[2]

The classical mechanism by which inflation is made impossible
at less-than-full employment is the assumed "mobility of resources."
Suppose there to be significant unemployment of labor somewhere in
the economy. And suppose labor at a particular location (or in a particular occupation) to be fully employed. Then an increase in the demand for output at that location (or requiring additional labor of that
type) would attract labor from those places (or occupations) where it
was presently unemployed, thereby relieving the temporary bottleneck
and providing additional supply to meet the new demand—thus preventing inflation.

Neoclassical economists explain the simultaneous existence of
inflation and unemployment with the aid of such modern concepts as
worker expectations and imperfect information. Government deficit
spending, expanded money supply, or "exogenous" increases in the
propensity to consume resulting (say) from optimistic expectations
will all increase the demand for output. This in itself will exert some
upward pressure on prices, according to the "elasticity of supply" of
the various goods or services.[3] In order to produce the additional
output, firms or offices or stores demand additional labor. This will
tend to drive up wages (or to increase the bargaining power of workers). But that in turn means increased costs of production which eventually get passed along to consumers in the form of higher prices.[4]

In the short run, prices (with their "head start") rise faster
than wages, output and employment grow, and it seems that additional
demand-driven inflation is "buying" us reduced unemployment. This
is the relationship embodied in the so-called Phillips curve, the well-
known inverse (downward-sloping) trade-off between the rate of change
of the price level and the level of unemployment.

Why don't prices fall back to their old level as supply rises to
meet the extra demand? Why, in other words, does supply apparently
adjust only with a lag, thereby maintaining at least some of the price
increase? This has been the subject of much research in labor economics during the past 10 years. The orthodox answer has to do with

the "job search" behavior of workers. In the first place, there may
be barriers to the immediate mobility of workers from one place (or
occupation) to another. Perhaps the unemployed workers lack the
skills, experience, or "attitudes" needed by those employers who are
trying to expand their activity.[5] Perhaps there is inadequate transportation to permit easy migration (or commuting) from places of
high employment to places of low unemployment. Or perhaps those
who are chronically unemployed are psychologically as well as technically incapable of performing the new work to be done, because, in
their insularity from the mainstream economy, they have come to
form a "culture of poverty" whose values and norms are inconsistent
with modern industrial/commercial life.

Some of the "search theorists" have concentrated on the behavior of workers themselves in their search for jobs. Workers are assumed to have in mind, at any point in time, a "reservation wage,"
the minimum wage rate beneath which they feel it undesirable (or un-
becoming, or even—given the availability of welfare or unemployment
insurance—unnecessary) to accept a job that is offered to them. It is
assumed that all unemployed workers have a certain expected worth
in the marketplace, according to their potential productivity, or value
to employers. The job search will continue as long as the reservation
wage exceeds this "opportunity wage"—as long as workers continue
to "price themselves out of the market." The longer the duration of
unemployment and search, the more the worker is forced to adjust his
or her expectations to reality. Finally, when expectations and real
possibilities become coincident, if there are job vacancies, then workers will become employed again—by choice.[6]

Since 1970, it appears that the inflation-unemployment trade-off
has worsened, that a higher rate of change of prices is associated with
any given level of unemployment. Some neoclassical economic theorists explain this by a process involving worker learning. Remember
that during the expansion following the demand increase, prices rise
before wages do. This means that real wages—purchasing power—are
initially declining. In an attempt to catch up, workers' unions exert
an exogenous demand for higher wages. By this time in the cycle,
government is probably reducing the deficit and/or the rate of growth
(or the price) of the money supply in order to halt the inflation. Together, these public and private actions will depress output and therefore employment, even as wages (and therefore prices) continue to
rise. Once the old real wage is restored (at its "equilibrium" level,
set by the prevailing level of productivity), the cycle ends—at an ab-
solutely higher level of prices and wages, but with the same real output, employment, and real wages as at the beginning, before the deficit spending or monetary expansion began. In one sense, the long-run

Phillips curve is a vertical line at the equilibrium level of unemployment. In another sense, there is no Phillips curve in the long run!

Other orthodox economists explain the apparent worsening of
the trade-off as a shifting out of the Phillips curve over time in response to the changing composition of the labor force. What is happening is a kind of statistical artifact. Suppose some given rate of
price increase tends to be associated with an unemployment rate of
2 percent for white adult males, the component of the labor force assumed by orthodox economists to have the most "human capital" and
therefore to be of the greatest value to employers. Suppose the average unemployment rate of nonwhite adult males is 6 percent. Then
measured adult male unemployment will be a weighted average of 2
percent and 6 percent, with the weights equal to the shares of the two
demographic groups in the total labor force. Now, suppose that the
nonwhite adult male share begins to rise. So long as workers continue
to face probabilities of employment that conform to the average for
their group, the weighted average unemployment rate for the economy
as a whole will necessarily rise. "Unemployment-prone" people make
up a larger share of the whole, so average unemployment rates must
go up—for any given level of aggregate demand, and so for any given
rate of inflation. Thus, the Phillips curve will seem to have shifted
out.

For 25 years, governments and their economic advisers have
used Keynesian fiscal and monetary policies to "stabilize" their economies. In practice, this has meant sliding up and down the Phillips
curve, periodically inflating and then deflating the economy, trading
off rising prices for rising unemployment and vice versa. With the
apparent worsening of the trade-off in recent years, the efficacy of
this approach (whatever one may think about its morality) has been
called into question. At the moment, it seems fair to say that orthodox economists do not know what to recommend, aside from continued
education, training, and investment in mobility-enhancement to facilitate the matching of unemployed workers and vacant jobs (tact, if not
charity, compels believers in the "culture of poverty" to keep their
own ideas about how to handle that "problem" to themselves).

There is no question that excess demand—where supplies are
inadequate to meet effective demands for them—will drive up prices
in a capitalist economy which uses prices as the basic mechanism for
rationing scarce goods and services. This holds, whether the excess
demand results from deliberate social policy or from unintended "acts
of God," whether demand increases relative to a given supply or supplies decline relative to given demands. President Johnson's decision
to go for both guns and butter without asking Congress for sufficient
taxation to finance both did create a major deficit that caused an excess demand for some goods and services. The dollar devaluations of

1971, 1972, and 1973, designed to protect our international credit and political/military influence, did increase the cost of imported goods. Soil bank programs and the artificial scarcity of wheat produced by the Russian wheat deal have driven up domestic prices. These ad hoc explanations of the current inflation are all valid. It is also true that women, youths, and nonwhites make up a larger proportion of the labor force than formerly.

On the other hand, a great deal of quantitative and qualitative research into the assumptions underlying the job search explanation for the Phillips curve—low technical "substitutability" of the unemployed for the employed, or lethargic "matching" of unemployed workers with vacant jobs, because of inadequate human capital or unrealistic expectations—has produced surprisingly little evidence in support of the theory.

Moreover, a rebirth of institutional studies into the structure of the "internal labor markets" inside firms, led by Michael Piore, has shown that wage structures are extraordinarily stable over time and exist largely independently of which workers occupy the jobs at any particular moment. There is little room for the kind of continuous individual wage "adjustments" posited by the neoclassicals.

It is my contention that supply and demand analysis is insufficient to explain the modern inflationary process. We also need to know what institutional forces lie behind supply and demand—the underlying political factors which shape the basic structure of the economy, within which prices are embedded.[7]

THE ABSENCE OF SYSTEMATIC PUBLIC PLANNING

Although the modern capitalist government is an active economic agent, its actions, especially in the United States, are still of a largely ad hoc nature. Long-range planning, outside of the military and related sectors, is not pursued with any conviction. John Kenneth Galbraith has written extensively on the contrast between private and public planning. I should like to revive an earlier Galbraith point which he seems to have disregarded of late, and to make one other point which seems to me to be an obvious consequence of no (or bad) public planning.

The early Galbraith point I have in mind involves the public goods/private goods problem. Market economies in general, and this one with a vengeance, systematically underproduce public goods (those things that involve some degree of collective consumption, like clean water) and overproduce those private goods which confer "external diseconomies"—unpriced or uncompensated costs—of one sort

or another. We use, in that felicitous Galbraithian phrase, "public
squalor to subsidize private affluence." The technical reasons for
this state of affairs have been well known to economists since the
1920s. Yet it seems to remain a matter for economics journals (and
mainly the footnotes of those!). Dealing with many of these "exter-
nalities" requires going outside the centralized marketplace. James
Buchanan has reminded us that the problem is not ended when we have
produced the public good; we must also operate such goods in a non-
market fashion or else suffer serious maintenance problems. In short,
we need planning. Inadequate (or deteriorated) supplies of public goods
and services are a major cause of the poor mobility or low productivity of capital as well as labor—witness the New England region's
problems with energy and transportation. Such bottlenecks can contribute to inflation in those expanding activities that require such "infrastructure" for their own operation.

But it is not only these chronic shortages of public goods that
contribute to structural inflation. There are also the unintended side
effects—including inflation in particular sectors—of unplanned ad-hoc-
type government actions. The United States takes a strong action,
such as the sale of millions of tons of wheat to the Soviet Union, as
part of detente policy. In doing so, it tied up thousands of railroad
freight cars in the Southwest, all commandeered to deliver wheat to
port for shipment to the Russians. Partly as a consequence, fertilizer
deliveries to ranchers and farmers are seriously delayed, contribut-
ing to shortages and low agricultural productivity, which eventually
translate into higher retail food prices.

LABOR MARKET SEGMENTATION

The search theorists are surely correct in their belief that labor immobilities contribute to increased costs of production. Their
error is in placing the source of this immobility primarily in the personal characteristics of the workers themselves, in their individual
behavior. And they treat as voluntary the process by which those
workers who are involuntarily "crowded" into the high unemployment
sector—what some of us call the "secondary labor market"—have
become socialized to work habits and norms which do not fit into the
employment conditions that characterize the "primary labor market,"
further inhibiting intersectoral mobility.

Other economists, working with tools developed in large part
by Piore and Peter Doeringer, see the barriers to mobility as far
more institutionalized, lying beyond the control of most workers
trapped in the secondary labor market. Work rules, wage bargains,

and hiring procedures in the primary labor market do not permit in-
stantaneous adjustment (including the hiring of migrants from the
secondary labor market) in response to pressure for change, because
such adjustment might upset politically sensitive and hard-won relative income and work responsibility arrangements. These are among
the forces which promote and reinforce the division of the economy
into labor market segments, with the property that (perhaps even in-
tergenerationally) mobility is greater within than among segments.

Segmentation is especially well defined along sex and race lines,
and Barbara Bergmann has postulated a process by which such discrimination in employment contributes to wage (and then price) inflation. As the economy expands, the labor market for white adult males
tightens first, until there is effectively ''full employment'' for that
privileged group. At this point, with additional vacancies appearing
or being created, many employers prefer to try to bid the already fully
employed white adult men away from their existing jobs rather than
to have to employ less-preferred women, Black, or young workers.
This raises the wages of the preferred group and (through the exercise of market power) the prices of the things they produce, even while
unemployment among other workers is still high. During economic
contractions, it is of course the women, Blacks, and youth who are
laid off first.

NATIONAL AND MULTINATIONAL OLIGOPOLY

To my mind, the most important systematic explanation of the
severity of modern capitalist inflation is the increasing power and influence (if not numerical incidence) of oligopoly—monopolistic concentration of production—throughout the capitalist world. It is concentrated employers who have the most market (i.e., price-making)
power, who can most easily influence their government regulators
(e.g., through promises of jobs at six-digit salaries), whose discrimination has the greatest consequences (because so many good jobs are
involved), who can afford to withhold output from the market, who can
(through their connections) anticipate government economic policies
and thereby change the conditions originally assumed by the policy
makers, and whose investment decisions are the most sensitive to
international opportunities for making a profit.

To be sure, our economy experiences some labor or other supply bottleneck inflation in one or another sector from time to time
(although, as I suggested earlier, even that is often attributable to the
lack of public planning—itself caused in large part by the opposition
of private corporations to public planning, at least in the United

States). And no one can escape occasional shortages due to real physical scarcities (although, again, planning could facilitate the process of substituting into less-scarce alternatives).

But overwhelmingly, we suffer from inflation which is sometimes caused—and is always exacerbated—by oligopoly. It works in three ways: (1) by profit-push—administered increases in price, often in anticipation of increased consumer spending; (2) by the extraction of government protection against price reductions;[8] and (3) by the vertical integration of entire industries, which eliminates external market exchange entirely in whole areas of the economy.

Orthodox economists are aware of at least some of the influences of oligopoly on inflation. The general tendency of oligopoly prices to rise quickly in response to (or in anticipation of) expanded demand but not to fall quickly (if at all!) in response to (or in anticipation of) declining demand imparts an upward bias to prices which has been recognized by Charles Schultze and Robert Solow (although neither of them seriously proposes action to weaken this oligopoly power).

In the 12-month period between October 1, 1973 and September 30, 1974, General Motors raised the average retail price of its cars 10 separate times, for an average increase of over $800. At the same time, its sales fell by 21 percent. To be sure, many of its costs rose significantly, notably labor (an additional cost of $2/hour since last year) and steel (an additional $65/ton since last fall). Nevertheless, faced with strong competition from other producers or from other transport modes, GM would have been forced to absorb some of these higher costs. That it did not—and padded the administered prices even further, by making standard some devices that were formerly optional, by building in "inflationary expectations," etc.— serves to remind us of the consequences of oligopoly.

Recently, Federal Trade Commission Chairman Lewis Engman announced his findings that "most regulated industries have become federal protectorates living in a cozy world of cost-plus, protected from the ugly specters of competitive efficiency and innovation." He pointed to decisions of the Civil Aeronautics Board, Interstate Commerce Commission, Department of Agriculture, and Federal Communications Commission: "Our airlines, our truckers, our railroads, our electronic media and countless others are on the dole. We get irate about welfare fraud, but our system of hidden regulatory subsidies makes welfare fraud look like petty larceny." Perhaps the two most dramatic examples in modern times concern the automobile industry's systematic destruction of potential competition from mass transit, and the oil industry's power to effect a drastic redistribution of income from labor to capital and reduce the future independence of consumers from the oil cartel.

The phenomena I have been discussing—weak public planning, labor market segmentation, and increasingly powerful oligopoly—are occurring in a setting of growing complexity. Some of the more fortunate of us could live with the excesses, mistakes, private decisions taken with total unconcern for external consequences, and sheer greed of private economic actors so long as the world was a simpler place. As that world becomes more complex—more technically and politically interdependent—it becomes harder and harder to live with these aspects of individualistic economic action.

THE SOCIAL AND PRIVATE CONSEQUENCES OF INFLATION

Suppose I am correct in arguing that it is a combination of the lack of serious public planning (too great a reliance on market pricing and the exercise of individual and interest group power), labor market segmentation, and increasingly powerful oligopoly that are responsible for the irreversibility of inflation in the United States? So what? Who suffers from inflation, anyway?

In the United States and the other developed capitalist countries, at least, inflation has not been sufficiently serious to undermine popular confidence in the currency and other institutions of those societies. The real issue is distributional: it is the costs of particular shortages or particular prices in particular places hurting particular groups that matter. On this score, I agree with a "conjecture" by Robert Solow:

> Look at the identity of the beneficiaries of these rather massive changes: the rest of us have transferred large amounts of real income to farmers, to owners of mineral deposits, to oil companies, Texas millionaires, and Middle Eastern potentates, and to foreigners generally . . .
> In the course of this inflation, . . . the winners have been narrow, peripheral groups, and the losers have been the broad blue-collar and white-collar, working class and middle class, urban industrial center of the economy. No wonder it feels to most of us that there have been only losers; we do not feel for the winners.[9]

That it is the changes in relative prices, rather than absolute general inflation as such, which bothers us is emphasized by Solow: "We [nonfarmers, non-oil millionaires, nonforeigners] would feel just as bad if the underlying price change had taken place around a stable price level, with no general inflation at all."

Solow believes that corporations gain in their share of the national income during inflations, relative to everyone else, because inflation is generally associated with expansion of production. Under such circumstances, large firms can exploit economies of scale which, at least in the short run, bring substantial profit increases. Leonard Rapping argues that it is labor's share which increases relative to the other actors in the game, because it is during expansionary periods that employers must have available and cooperative workers in order to realize those potential profits, so that labor's bargaining power increases.

The issue is surely much more complex than either economist is letting on. First, Barry Stein has developed evidence that the extent of economies of scale in major sectors of the American economy has been grossly exaggerated. Second, in any period of expanded demand for workers, organized labor will tend to benefit more than unorganized labor, so that while "factor shares" (the ratio of labor income to capital income) may become more equally distributed, the distribution of earnings could easily become more unequal (Peter Henle's well-known data are consistent with this argument). Third, white adult males will benefit more than others (a la Barbara Bergmann), due to discrimination. Since white adult males are far more likely to be unionized than others, these factors are closely correlated. Fourth, whether wages catch up with prices (even for the unionized workers in a position to negotiate from some kind of power base) also depends directly on government policy. The 1971-73 "freeze" froze wages far more effectively than prices (this doesn't surprise New York Times writer Eileen Shanahan: "Wage controls are somewhat self-enforcing, because managements seem happy to have Government-dictated limits on the wage increases they may give"). If President Ford tries to freeze both prices and wages this year, that seemingly "fair" policy will in fact institutionalize the worsening of real wages that has occurred since 1971.[10] And, finally, what happens to the distribution of real income depends on which sectors undergo the most serious inflation. Concentration in (and bad planning of) the food industry has seriously inflated retail food prices. Government "stabilization" policy (tight money now, after easier money in former years) has devastated the housing industry. And consumer/workers who have been socialized for over 25 years to stock up on energy-intensive durable goods of all kinds (while collectively consumed alternatives, such as mass transit and apartment houses with their shared services, were allowed to deteriorate and were not replaced sufficiently rapidly) now find that the cost of operating these goods—the cost of energy—is skyrocketing. In an inflation whose worst effects are in food, shelter, and energy, it is hard to believe that the distribution of real income is improving for the working class.

What is clear is that banks are a major loser in a general infla-tion.[11] They are the creditors who must continue to accept loan re-payments in devalued currency. It is they who inherit properties in default, which must often be managed rather than abandoned because they are occupied by increasingly well-organized tenants. It is they who must absorb much of the risk associated with the increased specu-lation in stocks, bonds, and currencies that general inflation both en-courages and makes possible under capitalism. No wonder, then, that bankers and their representatives in Washington wail the loudest about the dangers of ''rampant inflation'' and insist that we ''bite the bul-let'' and support deflationary policies at any cost.

CONCLUSION

Not even the Republican hierarchy disputes the contention that the recessions of 1970 and 1974 were deliberately planned in order to ''bite the bullet'' and ''whip inflation.'' But Democratic economists and their disciples needn't feel superior on this score; Phillips curve theory lends itself directly to such an approach by posing the question: What mix of inflation and unemployment do you want to have?

While the subject of inflation is complicated—general versus relative, who pays and who benefits, whether and how price inflation relates to wage inflation—there is nothing complicated about reces-sion. Unemployed workers do not add to social output. They do draw on transfer payments (welfare, unemployment compensation, etc.) which must be financed by all levels of government, even as the tax revenues for financing those payments dwindle. Families break up, neighborhoods deteriorate, drug and alcohol sales rise, property crime increases. Because of the conservative ''red-lining'' pro-pensities of private bankers, neighborhoods (and even whole regions) that once begin to decline during recessions are hard-pressed to raise the capital with which to turn themselves around later. It seems ab-solutely clear to me that the social consequences of recession are far greater than those of any inflation ever observed in any modern capitalist society.

In any case, such indirect attempts to induce deflation may be unnecessary. Why not deal with inflation directly, if indeed inflation is the major social problem that so many believe it to be? Galbraith has proposed a program that would consist of (1) wage, price, and profit controls on the largest corporations; (2) a ''social contract'' allowing wages to catch up to current prices enough to restore the real wage rate of some earlier year; (3) a surtax on high incomes, coupled with the closing of some loopholes; (4) selective credit allocation for housing; (5) expanded public service (and, one would hope, public works) employment grants from the federal government to state and local governments; (6) planned expansion of food and feed grains; and (7) a large excise tax on private automobiles, the proceeds to be used to finance mass transportation and a long-term infrastructure planning agency. Robert Solow has called for "a little well-aimed indexing," especially of the personal income tax, "so that inflation doesn't automatically increase the effective tax rate, especially on those near the bottom of the income scale."

Both Solow and James Tobin have warned against too ready an acceptance of the fear of inflation. The "double-digit inflation" scare-talk in the media may be similar to the anxiety over a possible $60 billion federal budget deficit. While large in absolute terms, such a deficit would be relatively smaller than the famous "Kennedy-Heller" deficit of 1962. Perhaps it is simply the scale that we fear. But then we are indeed in deep trouble. We need to manage our trillion-dollar-plus economy, not fear it. We cannot stand a loss of confidence at the discovery that the economy is much larger than it used to be.

In any case, I am not willing to sacrifice the goal of full employment for the sake of controlling inflation. Along with Solow, "I am not willing to bite this particular bullet." The fear of inflation should not be allowed to deter us in planning and executing a full employment policy in the United States.

NOTES

1. In order to finance increased deficits, the government must sell more bonds. Conservatives (especially those engaged in the marketing of private bonds) fear that this will reduce the availability of investable capital to the private sector, presumably because of the relatively lower risk of public bonds. These vested interests are among the most outspoken critics of "inflationary economic expansions."

2. Recent attempts by Bert Gross, Stan Moses, Thomas Vietorisz, the author, and others to expand the definition of the labor force to include underutilized or "discouraged" workers are relevant here. If the "true" labor force is larger than that which is now officially considered by the government, then the measured gap between potential and actual GNP is understated in official statistics. And that in turn leaves more "room" for deficit spending and expansionary monetary policy as noninflationary instruments for promoting full employment—provided, of course, that other (structural)

forces exacerbating inflation can be removed. The rest of this article
concerns those structural forces.

3. "Elasticity of supply" usually refers to the responsiveness
of producers—or distributors or sellers—to changes in the price they
can get for their product. A good or service in fairly fixed supply in
the short run, such as medical service, is said to be highly "price-
inelastic" in supply, so that increases in demand tend to translate into large increases in price, with little increase in the quantity sup-
plied.

4. Oligopolies—firms with economic and political power to set
(the technical term is "administer") their prices, in contrast with
competitive firms that can only charge "what the market will bear,"
i.e., the going price—can pass these cost increases along immediately.
Indeed, that may explain why they are so agreeable to large collective
bargaining wage settlements. But as labor cost increases diffuse
throughout the economy, becoming general cost increases, all firms
will face higher unit costs of production that necessitate higher prices
for given quantities of output.

5. It is important to distinguish, however, between employers'
needs that are intrinsic to the work to be done—e.g., manual dexterity
is technically important to being a plumber—and those that are arbi-
trarily set, perhaps because of custom, perhaps in order to screen
out technically competent but socially "undesirable" workers.

6. Most job searches are of fairly short duration. Thus, the
theory seemed to provide a plausible explanation of the important empirical discovery in the 1960s that high turnover—sporadic periods
of joblessness—is more typical than long-term "hard core" unemployment. There are other explanations, however, and I shall discuss
them later.

7. Thomas Vietorisz uses the metaphor of the bird cage to teach
the importance of the concept of "embedding," and to underscore the
Cambridge (U.K.) critique that neoclassical economics posits a more
or less self-contained economic system, whereas in fact the values
of "economic" variables are indeterminate without prior information
from the "outside." In Vietorisz's words: "Millions of unimportant
decisions are made every day in local markets—the soap film covering the wire frame of the bird cage. The really important decisions—
the wire frame itself—are less numerous, but far more fundamental.
And they are explained by an analysis of power, not competitive ad-
vantage." I want to address myself briefly to the wire frame.

8. There is no question that much regulatory activity does prevent prices from falling when demand for the product or service falls,
as a recent ABC-TV news analysis of the Interstate Commerce Commission and the Civil Aeronautics Board made all too clear.

But, as with inflation itself, it is necessary to ask: Who benefits from these "market imperfections," and how did they get there in the first place? Almost always, such rates were introduced—and are maintained—in order to satisfy one or another large and powerful corporate (and sometimes labor) interest group. Government regulation often does reinforce inflation in the sectors it "regulates," but in much the same ways (and for the same reasons) that private oligopoly promotes inflation of prices subject to "administration" by the oligopolists. It can hardly be attributed to "unbridled expansion of government at the expense of private industry"—a favorite conservative complaint.

9. Robert M. Solow, "The Intelligent Citizen's Guide to Inflation," The Public Interest, Winter 1975, p. 58.

10. In any case, as Frank Ackerman and Arthur MacEwan remind us, "A wage-price freeze automatically favors profits. As output per worker rises, but wages remain constant, the amount of product sold can increase while costs are unchanged. Rising sales revenues with constant costs mean increasing profits." In the absence of profit control, only if workers are allocated the full amount of their increased productivity, through appropriate wage increases, could a freeze be said to be equitable.

11. Particular sectors will suffer disproportionately according to the particular type of sectoral inflation experienced. The most prominent case is housing, which, in this country, is almost entirely dependent upon private capital financed in markets which are highly sensitive to federal interest rates. When the latter are raised, as part of an anti-inflation policy, housing starts invariably collapse. State and local governments suffer, also, but not from inflation so much as from simultaneous inflation and recession. At such times, revenues fall while costs rise. To attempt to reduce such unintended deficits by raising taxes may drive tax-paying households and firms out of the jurisdiction, thereby increasing the deficit! Floating bonds to finance deficit operating budgets is frowned upon by the private bond market, and can seriously impair a jurisdiction's ability to borrow for capital improvements at a later time.

7

RECONSTRUCTION IN NATIONAL ECONOMIC POLICY
Leon H. Keyserling

We are now in the longest and deepest economic downturn since the Great Crash in the 1930's. In April, 1975, full-time unemployment as customarily measured was 8.9 percent, or above 8 million. The full-time equivalent of part-time unemployment was 1.7 percent. The concealed unemployment, those discouraged from actively looking for jobs by scarcity of job opportunity, and therefore not officially counted as unemployed, was 1.2 percent. Thus, the true level of unemployment was 11.7 percent (discrepancy due to rounding), or more than 10.5 million.

Through the degree of our failure to maintain full employment and full production from 1953 forward, the deficiency in total national production (GNP) in first quarter 1975 was about $300 billion at an annual rate. And even if we write off as lost forever a substantial part of the larger gains in productivity which would have resulted from 1953 forward if we had enjoyed a fully used economy throughout, the economy in first quarter was operating at an annual rate about $215 billion below reasonably full production.

This in itself meant a loss of more than $50 billion in public revenues at all levels of government at existing tax rates. With these revenues, we would have just that much more to apply to the sorely starved priorities of our domestic needs—housing, education, and health services; mass transportation and energy development;

Originally published in Viewpoint 5, no. 2 (1975), pp. 2-8, and Challenge 18, no. 3 (July/August 1975), pp. 23-25, copyright © 1975 by International Arts and Sciences Press, Inc.

The Unemployment Cycles Since 1948
(quarterly data)

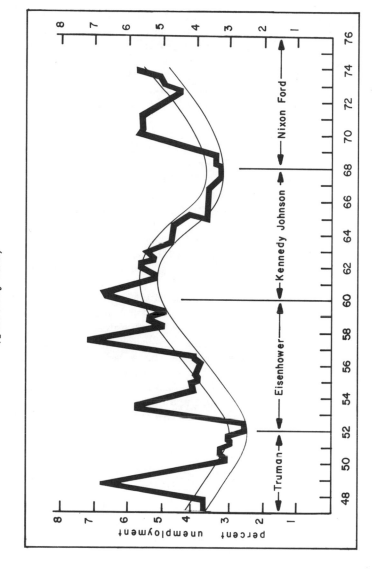

increases in other human well-being payments; income supports to
overcome poverty among those really unable to work; and a number
of other great domestic priorities requiring public outlays.

We cannot forge the programs and policies needed to lift us
from where we are now to where we ought to be, unless we recognize
that where we are now is neither new nor radically different in cause
or effects from the troubles we have had before. From 1953 to date,
we have five times repeated a fairly consistent pattern of inadequate
upturn, stagnation, and recession or absolute downturn. With some
ups and downs to be sure, we have in the long run moved further and
further away from full employment and full production. And the processes by which this has happened have been due to essentially the
same errors of analysis and defects in policy and program all along.

During the period 1953 through 1974 as a whole, we forfeited
more than $2.6 trillion worth of GNP (1974 dollars), and consequently
forfeited in the neighborhood of $700 billion of public revenues at all
levels which could have been put to very good use. Concurrently, we
suffered more than 54 million man-years of excessive unemployment,
true employment concept.

If we do not do much better in the future than we have done in
the past—and I see no prospect of doing much better without drastic
changes in national policies and programs—we will during 1976-1980
inclusive forfeit another $1.2 trillion of GNP and more than $300 billion of public revenues at all levels (1974 dollars), and experience
another 16.5 million man-years of excessive unemployment, true employment concept. The ratio of unemployment to GNP loss would not
be nearly as large as in the long past, because higher incomes and
other factors increase the number of dollars received by each employed worker. But another 16.5 million man-years of excessive unemployment would be intolerable and dangerous beyond description.

What must we now start to do, as we decide not to piddle but
to plan?

PURPOSEFUL PLANNING INSTEAD OF FORECASTS

The first error to correct is to substitute purposeful and planned goals for excessive emphasis upon pure forecasts. The President's January, 1975, Economic Report forecast 7.8 percent full-time
officially reported unemployment in 1976; 7.5 percent in 1977; 6.9
percent in 1978; and 6.8 in 1979. The new Budget Committees in the
Senate and the House forecast 7 to 7.5 percent full-time unemployment
at the end of 1976. Instead of resigning ourselves to these alarming
forecasts, we should at once set about resolutely to reduce full-time

or officially recorded unemployment to about 3 percent by the end of
1977. After that, we should set about to do still better. Through setting specific quantitative goals and devising means toward their attainment, the morbid forecasts of what is going to happen should be reversed instead of vindicated.

This task is difficult, but not beyond our capabilities. President
Roosevelt in early 1933, confronted by almost 13 million unemployed
or 24.9 percent of the civilian labor force, did not ask for forecasts.
Vigorous policies and programs were set in motion which cut unemployment about in half by early 1937. Thereafter through 1939, unemployment increased. But this was not because nobody knew what to do;
it was rather because conservative or reactionary forces grew strong
enough to prevent continuing what had been so well-started.

In 1939, unemployment was 9.5 million, or 17.2 percent of the
civilian labor force. By 1944 it was reduced to 670 thousand, or 1.2
percent. World War II in itself did not do this. It happened because
we recognized that jobs are more beneficial to individuals and to the
economy than unemployment. And it was no easier to attain full employment through the process of making weapons of destruction than
to attain it now through the happier process of meeting essential domestic needs.

President Truman, whom I served as Chairman of the Council
of Economic Advisers, never asked me to forecast unemployment. He
dedicated himself to the achievement of full employment, and by 1953
full-time unemployment was only 2.9 percent. Again, this was not just
because of the Korean war. In 1972, when the Vietnam war was in full
swing, full-time unemployment was 5.9 percent of the civilian labor
force.

Full-time unemployment in 1961 was 6.7 percent, in consequence
of the policies of the Eisenhower Administration during eight years.
President Kennedy did not ask for forecasts; he commenced action,
and President Johnson continued it. By 1969, unemployment was 3.5
percent.

Let us now turn to an examination of where national policies
and programs have gone wrong, as a foundation for developing cor-
rective measures.

MANAGEMENT OF THE PROBLEM OF INFLATION

A second reason why we have done so badly is that stagnations
and recessions have been repeatedly contrived, responsive to the
"trade-off" theory that higher employment and greater resource use
bring more inflation, and that higher unemployment and more deficient

resource use bring less inflation. Even today, an adequate program of economic restoration is being estopped by this false theory.

It is unconscionable that the full-time equivalent of more than 10.5 million breadwinners and their families suffer the distress and humiliation of unemployment, in order (hypothetically) that Mr. Keyserling may be able to buy a third car or another steak banquet for somewhat less than if unemployment were one-third or one-fourth that amount. More important, the empirical evidence for more than 20 years is that a healthy economy generates far less price inflation than a sick economy.

During the Truman years, 1947-1953, the average annual rate of real economic growth was 4.9 percent. Full-time unemployment averaged 4.0 percent and, as earlier stated, was reduced to 2.9 percent in the last year. Average annual inflation, despite the Korean war during almost half the time, was 3 percent, and was reduced to 0.8 percent during the last year. In vivid contrast, during the Nixon-Ford years 1969-1974, the real average annual rate of economic growth was only 2.5 percent. Full-time unemployment averaged 5.1 percent, and was 5.6 percent in the last year. Inflation averaged 6.1 percent, and rose to 12.2 in the last year.

The most poignant example was from first quarter 1974 to first quarter 1975. The real economic growth rate was minus 5.8 percent. Full-time unemployment was 6.2 percent, and as earlier stated rose to 8.9 percent in April, 1975. The rate of price inflation was 11.2 percent.

The very recent reduction in the inflation rate from more than 13 percent to about 8 percent is not properly attributable to the false claim that this happened because we have continued to accept an intolerable amount of unemployment. It is rather because some of the transitory factors generating double-digit inflation have disappeared or waned. We would never have gotten up to 13 percent or even 8 percent inflation if we had maintained a healthy economy, and the surest and best way to reduce inflation much further is to restore a fully healthy economy as rapidly as feasible. Under the goals and programs I recommend, I estimate that inflation might be reduced to 3 percent by the end of 1977.

THE TRUE FUNCTION OF PRICES HAS BEEN OVERLOOKED

The third reason for our troubles is that the true function of prices has been misinterpreted. Our real wealth and well-being are not determined by price trends per se, but rather by how close we come to full use of our resources, social justice in the allocation of resources and incomes, and taking care of the great priorities of our needs. Historically, rising, stable, or falling price trends have been contributory or inimical to these three great purposes, depending upon whether these price trends within the complex of other trends and policies have worked toward or against these great purposes in terms of the relationships between price trends and other trends.

The problem is basically distributive. For example, during most upturn periods, we have had profit-investment inflation and a lag in wages and other consumer incomes. If the actual price increases since 1969 had been in the context of policies successfully designed to achieve the great purposes, we would have made an acceptable bargain. But these same price increases, accompanied and augmented by national policies designed to maldistribute incomes and resources and thus to thwart these three great purposes, have been a cruel, indefensible, and stupid inflation. Such policies certainly ignore the true function of prices.

MISUSE OF KEYNESIAN ECONOMICS

The fourth persistent error has been the distorted use of the Keynesian economics in an aggregative or blunderbus manner to stimulate the economy when it is too slack, and restrain it when it is too tight. This approach feeds the fat and starves the lean. For, in fact, a deficiency or excess in total demand is due primarily to misallocations of resource use and incomes which destroy the balance essential to optimum performance. We must simultaneously restrain relative excesses in some parts of the economy and overcome relative shortfalls in other sectors. As already stated, the U.S. economic problem is essentially distributive, and current policies are not paying enough attention to this. Some still move in the opposite direction.

THE FALSE DICHOTOMY BETWEEN
ECONOMIC AND SOCIAL GOALS

The fifth cardinal error is adherence to a false dichotomy between purely economic objectives and fulfillment of the priorities of our human and social needs. Even if vindication of these needs imported a somewhat lower rate of economic growth, we have become rich enough to value justice and human decency above progress narrowly conceived. However, under current and prospective technological conditions, the improved distribution of income, and the relative as well as the absolute enlargement of services to human welfare, are the foremost requirements for a fully used economy in conventional terms.

THE PROBLEM OF THE SELECTIVE SHORTAGES

The sixth important error is the prevalent thinking about selective shortages. Despite the actions of the Arabs, the shortages of energy, which include not only oil but also gas and electricity, have become critical rather than merely inconvenient because during long years we have not planned to expand energy in accord with full economic needs; actually, we have deliberately reduced energy expansion because we did not have nor even aspire to a full economy.

Critical shortages of food have not resulted because of a few "crop failures." Instead, for 20 years or longer, national farm policy followed the false dogma that we were "overproducing" food, even while millions of Americans were malnourished, while we were exporting too little food to fight starvation elsewhere, and while millions of farm people were transferred to urban unemployment. In addition, domestic food and fiber consumption would have been much higher if income distribution had been better, and if the economy had been full. The shortages of mass transportation have been due primarily to the scarcity philosophy of the railroads, promoted rather than prohibited by such national policies as the approval of the Penn-Central merger. We have had shortages by misconception or neglect; not abundance through planning.

Even today, there are no shortages which should prevent us from moving toward full employment and full production by the end of 1977. And the shifts in the pattern of production and employment which are essential to this basic objective would be energy conserving, i.e., shifting more employment and production toward housing, mass transportation, educational and health services, and anti-pollution efforts.

THE FEDERAL BUDGET AND THE NATIONAL ECONOMY

The seventh error is that unfounded concern about the immediate size of the Federal deficit stands in the way of the needed stimulative measures. Recent pronouncements of the new Committees on the Budget in the Senate and the House do not set even tolerable goals for production, employment, and service of priority needs, and then shape the budget as one of many instruments to be attuned to these ends. Instead, these Committees have first decided what the budget and the deficit should be, and then resigned themselves to the miserable production, employment, and priority results which a budget of this type and size promotes.

THE LOGISTICS OF THE ECONOMIC PROBLEM

The eighth error, and in some ways the most important today, is the neglect of the logistics of the economic restoration task. As already stated, the economy today is running at an annual rate about $215 billion below reasonably full resource use. And toward achieving this reasonably full use and full employment by the end of 1977, we need an expansion of $295 billion in the annual total national production between now and 1977 as a whole. This goal is in 1974 dollars; it would be considerably higher in current dollars. We need to increase civilian employment by 8.4 million for 1977 as a whole.

THE NEED FOR A WIDER RANGE OF INTEGRATED POLICIES

The ninth error is excessive reliance upon fiscal policy. No fiscal policy, even if correct, can achieve the needed results if monetary policy continues to lean heavily in the opposite direction. And many other national policies need to be joined in the drive for a full and just economy. This includes, among others, social insurance, housing, agriculture, energy, mass transportation, and income distribution. We now have a confused medly of policies and programs, but no coherent policy or program.

THE NEEDED PLANNING EFFORT

Under the Employment Act of 1946, the President should set forth, for the guidance of all Executive programs and for submission to the Congress, a short-range and long-range program (under planning, the two are essentially one) directed toward restoration of full employment, production, and purchasing power by the end of 1977. These goals should relate not only to the volume of activity, but also to priority programs and the enlargement of social justice. They

should involve broad quantitative analysis of the needed amount and
distribution of purchasing power, both private and public, with appropriate stress upon equitable considerations.

The federal government, of course, would not fulfill all of these
objectives. It would instead provide a perspective for the mutual efforts of private enterprise, voluntary associations, and governments
at all levels. But the federal government would meet its bedrock responsibility to close the gap between these goals and what others do,
and toward this end would fuse its manifold economic and social programs into a unified and consistent policy and program. These efforts
must include, by legislation if necessary, changes in the policies of
the Federal Reserve System to bring them to the support of the vital
goals and policies to be set forth in the Economic Report of the President.

For reasons already set forth, I believe that these approaches
are the best way to reduce inflation, and would prevent an unbalanced
preoccupation with inflation as the top problem from turning us away
from even more essential goals and giving us horrendous inflation to
boot. But if controls equitably applied are needed for a time, they
should be used, recalling that these worked effectively when they were
sincerely and intelligently evoked.

The Hawkins-Humphrey Equal Opportunity and Full Employment
Bill, introduced last year and now under active consideration in improved form as H.R. 50, makes a large start in these directions. That
measure, and the testimony thus far offered, are worthy of the attention of all concerned with where we are now and need to go.

The main elements in H.R. 50, which is rapidly gaining important support, are the following.

Employment Goals

1. The measure, if enacted, would write into law the responsibility of our federal government to create an economic environment
in which, with private enterprise, voluntary associations, and state
and local governments doing their full share, the federal government
would recognize its bedrock and ultimate responsibility to guarantee
the right to useful employment at appropriate pay for all those able
and willing to work, plus those who can be brought up to this level.
The President, under the Employment Act of 1946, would be mandated
to bring forth and send to the Congress immediate policies and programs (allowing for nonfederal efforts) to reduce full-time unemployment as officially measured to 3 percent—less than 3 million—within
eighteen to twenty months after enactment of the legislation, and much

more later on. (We reduced unemployment to 1 percent in 1944.) The measure also provides that immediate efforts be started, through supplementary reservoirs of private and public employment projects, to help all others to whom the guarantee of the right to work would apply, even when unemployment has reached the 3 percent level. Scarcity of workers is better than scarcity of jobs.

Distributive Goals

2. The President would also be required under the Employment Act to transmit to the Congress from year to year an updated set of policies and programs as part of a Full Employment and National Purposes Budget. In addition to specified quantitative goals for full employment, production, and purchasing power, the Purposes Budget would include goals for the composition and distribution of income and output conducive to sustained full employment, production, and purchasing power. To date, this equilibrium analysis has been grossly neglected and, without it, national policies and programs are flying blind.

3. A salient defect in action under the Employment Act of 1946 has been excessive concentration upon general or aggressive fiscal policies, as well as upon the same kinds of monetary policies. This approach has severely neglected, at the individual or structural level, the wide range of priority programs which, under the impact of technological trends, are absolutely essential to sustained full employment, production, and purchasing power. They are equally essential to the extirpation of poverty and other excessively low incomes, to the servicing of urgent national needs, and to the attainment of distributive and social justice. And this oversight has usually been accompanied by the refrain that such programs "cannot be afforded" and are not of major concern to economists serving under the Employment Act. The Hawkins-Humphrey bill mandates that such priority programs be budgeted and proposed to the Congress under the Purposes Budget.

The Purposes Budget would therefore include short-range and long-range goals for conservation and development of natural resources and raw materials and energy supply; decent housing for all; improvement of the environment; adequate medical care for all; full educational opportunity for all, accompanied by adequate day care and nursery and kindergarten facilities; mass transportation; a full-economy production level of food and fibers; nation-wide equalization efforts with respect to incomes and public services; development of basic and applied science; artistic, aesthetic, cultural, and recreational activities; federal aid to state and local governments for needed public goods and services; virtual liquidation of poverty, substandard wages, and substandard conditions of employment in the United States, and substantial income progress among low-income families above the poverty level who still live in deprivation; needed increases in income transfer expenditures and related services for those unable to work and their dependents; promotion of small business and competitive enterprise, and action against practices by businesses of any size which are clearly inimical to the public interest; appropriate national defense, space exploration, international cooperation, and aid to the underdeveloped countries; and substitute activities to facilitate or adjust for reductions in military and other industrial activities.

Obviously, all of these goals, on both a short-range and a long-range basis, would be integrated and balanced in terms of our growing needs and capabilities. This is the hallmark of planning. Clearly, the measure does not define the desirable size of most of these programs; that is left to the President and the Congress to specify and help to achieve under a continuous planning process at the highest levels of public responsibility.

4. The practice of national policy under the Employment Act has not only been to neglect these priority programs grievously in the long run, but also to restrain them first and foremost whenever the economy is deemed (usually erroneously) to be "under too much pressure." This restraint exists even today, when the economy is suffering from tremendous slack. The Hawkins-Humphrey measure would mandate that these priority programs be budgeted continuously at the appropriate level of our full employment and production capabilities. When the economy is very slack, such action would also have powerful restorative effects. When the economy is too tight—which is unlikely in the foreseeable future—these priorities should not be sacrificed; instead, progressive tax policies should be used to cut back on superfluous or deferrable demand elsewhere in the economy. This is how Keynesian economics should really be applied.

Federal Budget Policies and Control of Inflation

5. H.R. 50 also proposes a legislative finding that attempts to balance the federal budget at the expense of the national economy are costly beyond description to the economy and the people, and are sure to result in stupendous federal deficits. The stated objective is to balance the budget at full employment, or even to have a "full-employment surplus" budget.

6. In addition to primary reliance upon reasonably full resource use to restrain inflation, this "full-employment surplus" budget would be used as the primary weapon against classical or excess-demand inflation, and the measure prohibits contrived unemployment and economic slack in the effort to curb inflation. However, the bill specifies certain counter-inflation devices, including controls when needed, to deal with other, more usual manifestations of inflation, such as those in "administered price" areas.

Monetary Policy

7. Since 1953, the policies of the "independent" Federal Reserve Board have brought on recurrent recessions, have stunted priority programs, and have redistributed more than 800 billion dollars regressively through excessively high interest rates. The Hawkins-Humphrey measure provides means whereby FRB policies would be brought into accord with the purposes of the bill, including enlarged congressional and presidential participation in monetary policy. It is a strange anachronism for our central banking system to be entirely "independent."

Reservoirs of Employment Projects

8. To supplement the overall program for full employment and priorities as defined above, the Hawkins-Humphrey measure would assure full employment to all eligible and willing to work through a nationwide and reasonable decentralized reservoir of public and private employment projects, carefully integrated with the priority public investments referred to above. This would utilize such instrumentalities as a new U.S. Full Employment Service (expanding the responsibilities of the U.S. Employment Service), a Job Guarantee Office, and a Standby Job Corps, plus enlarged use of local planning councils. However, the Purposes Budget would serve to guide the preponderance of public investment toward high priority programs of enduring value which reflect long-range needs. The increased success of action under the Purposes Budget would guard against the proliferation of hastily devised supplementary employment programs.

Organization for the Effort

9. The Hawkins-Humphrey bill would fix concentrated responsibility with the President, under the Employment Act, to perform the tasks set forth above, including recommendations to the Congress. We need, I believe, mandated purposes and programs under a planned effort more than we need additional federal agencies. However, the working relationships between a properly restaffed Council of Economic Advisers and the specialized federal agencies of large size are broadened and specifically defined, so that these agencies may effectively perform their share of the required tasks. Correspondingly, the measure would enlarge the responsibilities of the Joint Economic Committee in the Congress, so that it may be restored to its originally intended function of providing guidelines to the Congress at large and to the various legislative and budget committees with respect to national action under the Hawkins-Humphrey measure. A broadly representative Advisory Council on Full Employment and National Purposes would be established, with a membership not limited to economists, to meet and consult with the President and the Council of Economic Advisers. For the purpose of annual conferences, an appropriately constituted advisory group would be attached to the Joint Economic Committee as well. This group would be mandated to hold public hearings in various labor market areas.

We must start at once to lift the floor of "political feasibility" to the level of what we must do to prosper and live in domestic tranquility. If those dedicated to this course play their part in a nationwide educational effort, many of us believe that the Hawkins-Humphrey bill, further improved, can become law before the end of 1976. And this would be a splendid way to increase the meaningfulness of celebrating our 200 years as a great and aspiring nation and people.

BOOKS

Abbati, Alfred Henry. Towards Full Employment. London: Basker-
ville Press, 1945.

Academy for Contemporary Problems, and National Conference on
Public Service Employment. Proceedings of a Conference on
Full Employment Without Inflation; November 2-3, 1974. Colum-
bus, Ohio: Academy for Contemporary Problems, 1975.

Angell, Sir Norman, and Wright, Harold. Can Governments Cure Unemployment? London and Toronto: J. M. Dent & Sons, 1931.

Bailey, Stephen K. Congress Makes A Law: The Story Behind the
Employment Act of 1946. New York: Columbia University Press,
1950.

_____. Roosevelt and His New Deal. London, 1938.

Baruch, Bernard M. American Industry in the War: A Report of the
War Industries Board. New York: Prentice-Hall, 1941.

Bellamy, Edward. Looking Backward: 2000-1887. New York:
Houghton Mifflin, 1887.

Berg, Ivar. Education and Jobs: The Great Training Robbery. New
York: Praeger Publishers, 1970.

Berkovits, Eugen. The Key to Full Employment Without Regimentation. New York: Longmans, Green, & Co., 1945.

_____. The Mechanics of Full Production and Full Employment:
A Solution to Depression. New York and Chicago: Wilcox &
Follett, 1946.

Beveridge, William H. Full Employment in a Free Society. New York:
W. W. Norton, 1945.

Blair, John M. Economic Concentration: Structure, Behavior, and
Public Policy. New York: Harcourt, Brace & World, 1972.

Bolino, A. C. Manpower and the City. Cambridge, Mass.: Schenkman, 1969.

Bowen, William G. and Finegan, T. A. The Economics of Labor Force Participation. Princeton, N.J.: Princeton University Press, 1969.

Bowen, William G., and Harbison, Frederick H. Unemployment In A Prosperous Economy: A Report of the Princeton Manpower Symposium. Princeton, N.J.: Woodrow Wilson School of Public and International Affairs, 1965.

Brayshaw, Shipley Neave. Post-War Employment For All. London: G. Allen & Unwin, 1942.

Bullock, Paul, ed. A Full Employment Policy for America. Los Angeles: University of California Manpower Research Center, 1974.

Burns, Arthur E., and Williams, Edward A. Federal Work, Security, and Relief Programs, WPA Research Monograph XXIV. 1941. Reprint. New York: Da Capo Press, 1971.

Burns, Arthur F., and Samuelson, Paul A. Full Employment Guide-posts and Economic Stability. Washington, D.C.: American Enterprise Institute for Public Policy Research, 1967.

Casselman, Paul Herbert. Economics of Employment and Unemployment. Washington, D.C.: Public Affairs Press, 1955.

Cassell, Frank H. The Public Employment Service: Organization in Change. Ann Arbor, Mich.: Academic Publications, 1968.

Clark, John Maurice. Economics of Planning Public Works. Washington, D.C.: U.S. Government Printing Office, 1935.

Cloward, Richard, and Piven, Frances Scott. Regulating the Poor. New York: Pantheon, 1971.

Cole, George Douglas Howard. The Means to Full Employment. London: V. Gollancz, 1943.

Copeland, Morris Albert. Toward Full Employment in Our Free Enterprise Economy. New York: Fordham University Press, 1966.

Copland, Sir Douglas Berry. The Road to High Employment: Admin-
    istrative Controls in a Free Economy. Cambridge, Mass.:
    Harvard University Press, 1945.

Culbertson, John M. Full Employment or Stagnation? New York:
    McGraw-Hill, 1964.

Curtis, Thomas Bradford. 87 Million Jobs: A Dynamic Program to
    End Unemployment. New York: Duell, Sloan, and Pearce, 1962.

Dennison, Henry Sturgis, et. al. Towards Full Employment. New
    York: McGraw-Hill, 1938.

Durand, John D. The Labor Force in the United States 1890-1960.
    New York: Social Service Research Council, 1948.

Ezekiel, Mordecai. Jobs for All: Through Industrial Expansion. New
    York: Alfred A. Knopf, 1939.

Feldman, Herman. The Regularization of Employment: A Study in
    the Prevention of Unemployment. New York: Harper & Bros.,
    1925.

Fellner, William John. Monetary Policies and Full Employment.
    Berkeley and Los Angeles: University of California Press, 1947.

Fitch, Lyle, ed. Planning For Jobs. Philadelphia and Toronto:
    Blakiston, 1946.

Full Employment League. How to Create More Jobs; A Sound Full
    Employment Program. New York: Full Employment League,
    1945.

Galbraith, John Kenneth. Economics and the Public Purpose. Boston:
    Houghton Mifflin, 1973.

_____. The New Industrial State. New York: Signet Books, 1967.

Gartner, Alan; Nixon, Russell A.; and Riessman, Frank, eds. Public
    Service Employment: An Analysis of Its History, Problems, and
    Prospects. New York: Praeger, 1973.

Gartner, Alan, and Riessman, Frank. The Service Society and the
    Consumer Vanguard. New York: Harper & Row, 1974.

Gilbert, Richard, et al. An Economic Program for American Democracy. New York: Vanguard, 1938.

Glyn, Andrew, and Sutcliffe, Robert. Capitalism in Crisis. New York: Pantheon, 1972.

Gordon, David M. Theories of Poverty and Discrimination. Lexington, Massachusetts: Heath Lexington Books, 1972.

Gordon, Robert Aaron. The Goal of Full Employment. New York: Wiley and Sons, 1967.

Gordon, Robert Aaron, and Margaret S., eds. Conference on Unemployment and the American Economy. New York: Wiley & Sons, 1966.

Grayson, Henry. Economic Planning Under Free Enterprise. New York: Public Affairs Press, n. d.

Greenleigh Associates. A Public Employment Program for the Unemployed Poor. New York: Greenleigh Associates, 1965.

Gruber, Karl. Conditions of Full Employment. Translated by Jean Meyer. London: W. Hodge & Co., 1952.

Hansen, Alvin Harvey. Economic Policy and Full Employment. New York: McGraw-Hill, 1947.

Haveman, Robert H. Unemployment, Idle Capacity, and the Evaluation of Public Expenditures. Baltimore: Johns Hopkins Press, 1968.

Jevons, H. Stanley. The Causes of Unemployment. London: Alabaster, Passmore & Sons, 1909.

Jones, David Caradog, ed. Full Employment and State Control: A Symposium on the Degree of Control Essential. London: J. Cape, 1945.

Jordon, Virgil. Full Employment and Freedom in America. New York, 1945.

Kalecki, Michael. The Last Phase in the Transformation of Capitalism. New York: Monthly Review Press, 1972.

Keller, Kent Ellsworth. Prosperity Through Employment: A Job For
    Every Man and Woman Who Wants to Work. New York and London:
    Harper & Brothers, 1936.

Keynes, J. M. The General Theory of Employment, Interest and
    Money. New York: Harcourt, 1936.

Kingdon, Frank. An Uncommon Man: Henry Wallace and 60 Million
    Jobs. New York: The Readers Press, 1945.

Large, Thomas. How To End Unemployment. London: J. Bale Sons,
    1930.

Lebergott, Stanley, ed. Men Without Work: The Economics of Unem-
    ployment. Englewood Cliffs, N.J.: Prentice-Hall, 1964.

Lecht, Leonard A. Changes in National Priorities During the 1960's:
    Their Implications for 1980. Washington, D.C.: National Planning
    Association, 1972.

Lekachman, Robert. The Age of Keynes. New York: Random House,
    1966.

Lerner, Abba, and Graham, Frank, eds. Planning and Paying for Full
    Employment. Princeton: Princeton University Press, 1946.

Levinson, Charles. Capital, Inflation, and the Multinationals. New
    York: Macmillan, 1971.

Long, Clarence D. The Labor Force in War and Transition. New
    York: National Bureau of Economic Research, 1952.

Lumer, Hyman. Is Full Employment Possible? New York: New
    Century Publications, 1962.

Lundberg, Erik, et al. Wages Policy Under Full Employment. Edited
    and Translated by Ralph Turvey. London: Hodge, 1952.

Mangum, Garth. The Emergence of Manpower Policy. New York:
    Holt, Rinehart & Winston, 1969.

Meadows, D., et. al. The Limits to Growth: A Report for the Club of
    Rome's Project on the Predicament of Mankind. New York:
    Universe Books, 1972.

Myrdal, Gunnar. The Challenge of World Poverty. New York: Pantheon Books, 1970.

National Commission on the Causes and Prevention of Violence. To Establish Justice, To Insure Domestic Tranquility. Washington, D.C.: National Commission on the Causes and Prevention of Violence, 1969.

National Commission on Technology, Automation, and Economic Progress. Technology and the American Economy. Washington, D.C.: U.S. Government Printing Office, 1966.

National Federation for Constitutional Liberties. Full Employment As a Safeguard to Civil Liberties. New York: National Federation for Constitutional Liberties, 1946.

National Resources Committee. The Structure of the American Economy: Part I; Basic Characteristics. Washington, D.C.: National Resources Committee, 1939.

O'Toole, James, et. al. Work in America. Cambridge, Mass.: MIT Press, 1973.

Oxford University, Institute of Statistics. The Economics of Full Employment: Six Studies in Applied Economics. Oxford: B. Blackwell, 1944.

Palmer, John Logan. Inflation, Unemployment, and Poverty. Lexington, Mass.: Lexington Books, 1973.

Pierson, John H.G. Full Employment. New Haven: Yale University Press, 1941.

_____. Full Employment in Practice. New York: New York University Press, 1946.

_____. Insuring Full Employment: A United States Policy for Domestic Prosperity and World Development. New York: Viking Press, 1964.

Polanyi, Michael. Full Employment and Free Trade. Cambridge: The University Press, 1945.

Reubens, Beatrice G. The Hard to Employ: European Programs. New York: Columbia University Press, 1970.

Robinson, Joan. The Problem of Full Employment: An Outline for Study Circles. London: Workers Educational Association, 1944.

Ropke, Wilhelm. The Economics of Full Employment: An Analysis of the United Nations' Report on National and International Measures for Full Employment. New York: American Enterprise Association, 1952.

Ross, Arthur M., ed. Employment Policy and the Labor Market. Berkeley and Los Angeles: University of California Press, 1965.

_____. Unemployment and the American Economy. New York: Wiley & Sons, 1964.

Schlesinger, Arthur M. The Age of Roosevelt: Volume 2; The Coming of the New Deal. Boston: Houghton Mifflin, 1959.

Schumpeter, Joseph A. History of Economic Analysis. New York: Oxford University Press, 1954.

Shannon, David A., ed. The Great Depression. Englewood Cliffs, N.J.: Prentice-Hall, 1960.

Sheppard, Harold L.; Harrison, Bennett; and Spring, William, eds. The Political Economy of Public Service Employment. Lexington, Mass.: D. C. Heath, 1972.

Siegel, Irving H. Fuller Employment With Less Inflation. Kalamazoo, Mich.: W. E. Upjohn Institute for Employment Research, 1969.

Solow, Robert M. The Nature and Sources of Unemployment in the United States. Stockholm: Almqvist & Wiksell, 1964.

Special Task Force to the Secretary of Health, Education, and Welfare. Work in America. Washington, D.C.: U.S. Government Printing Office, 1972.

Stead, William Henry. Democracy Against Unemployment: An Analysis of the Major Problem of Postwar Democracy. New York and London: Harper & Bros., 1942.

Stein, Herbert. The Fiscal Revolution in America. Chicago: University of Chicago Press, 1969.

Stemons, James S. Unemployment—Social Madness; Full Employment—Now and Forever. New York: William Frederick Press, 1946.

Terkel, Studs. Working. New York: Pantheon, 1974.

Turvey, Ralph, ed. & trans. Wages Policy Under Full Employment. London: W. Hodge, 1952.

Universities-National Bureau Committee for Economic Research. Policies To Combat Depression. Princeton, N.J.: Princeton University Press, 1956.

Vaizey, John. The Trade Unionist and Full Employment. London: Workers Education Association, 1955.

Wallace, Henry A. Sixty Million Jobs. New York: Reynal and Hitchcock, Simon & Schuster, 1945.

Wernette, John Philip. Financing Full Employment. Cambridge, Mass., 1945.

Winternitz, J. The Problem of Full Employment: A Marxist Analysis. London: Lawrence & Wishart, 1947.

Wolfbein, Seymour L. Education and Training for Full Employment. New York: Columbia University Press, 1967.

_____. Employment and Unemployment in the United States: A Study of the American Labor Force. Chicago: Science Research Associates, 1964.

Worcester, Dean Amory. Beyond Welfare and Full Employment: The Economics of Optimal Employment Without Inflation. Lexington, Mass.: Heath-Lexington Books, 1972.

ARTICLES

Abel, I. W. "Jobs Now!" Viewpoint 5, no. 2 (1975): 1.

Aberman, Sidney. "Towards Full Employment." Commonweal, November 9, 1945, pp. 90-92.

Abraham, William J., and Jaffee, A. J. "A Note on Alternative Measures of Unemployment and the Shortfall in Employment." New York Statistician, May/June 1972.

Ackley, Gardner, et. al. "The Employment Act After Twenty Years: The Legal Basis for Managing the Economy." George Washington Law Review 35 (1966): 169-392.

AFL-CIO. "America's Need: Social Services and Jobs." American Federationist 70, no. 8 (1963): 1-7.

_____. "The Specter of Rising Unemployment." American Federationist 69, no. 10 (1962): 12-18.

Allen, Clark Lee. "Are National Full Employment Policies Consistent with Freer Trade?" Nebraska Journal of Economics and Business 8, no. 1 (1968): 3-15.

American Economic Association. "Problems of Achieving and Maintaining Full Employment [Addresses before the American Economic Association, Washington, D.C., December 28-30, 1959]." American Economic Review 50, no. 2 (1960): 130-71.

_____. "Stabilizing the Economy: The Employment Act of 1946 in Operation [Addresses before the annual meeting of the American Economic Association, New York, December 28, 1949]." American Economic Review 40, no. 2 (1950).

Anderson, Bernard E. "Full Employment and Economic Equality." Annals of the American Academy of Political and Social Science 418 (1975): 127-36.

"An Economic Review of the Employment Act of 1946." Monthly Labor Review 80 (1957): 161-65.

Arles, J. P. "Emergency Employment Schemes: Job Creation Programs Under the International Labor Organization." International Labour Review 109 (1974): 69-88.

Ayres, B. Drummond, Jr. "3,000 Seek Jobs in Atlanta Melee." New York Times, January 10, 1975.

Bach, G. L. "Price Stability and Full Employment Too?" Harvard Business Review 49, no. 5 (1971): 68-78.

Baerwald, Friedrich. "Implications of Full Employment." America 73 (1945): 448-49.

Barnes, Leo. "The Anatomy of Full Employment." Nation 160 (1945): 593-97.

Barnes, Peter. "Jobs: Prospects for Full Employment." Working Papers for a New Society 3, no. 3 (1975): 49-58.

Bell, Carolyn Shaw. "Age, Sex, Marriage and Jobs." The Public Interest, no. 30 (1973): 76-87.

Benoit-Smullyan, Emile. "Full Employment: Its Economic and Legal Aspects." Antioch Review 5 (1945): 320-34.

_____. "On the Meaning of Full Employment." Review of Economics and Statistics 30 (1948): 127-34.

Berman, Lewis. "The Slow Road Back To Full Employment." Fortune, June 1975, pp. 84ff.

Bolino, August C. "Manpower Development: Charges and Challenges Under the Manpower Development and Training Act of 1962." Michigan Business Review, July 1965.

Braunthal, Alfred. "Wage Policy and Full Employment." International Postwar Problems 3 (1946): 31-50.

Briggs, Carson, and Riessman, Frank. "They're Throwing the Wrong Curve: Workers Pay for Inflation Fears." Viewpoint 5, no. 2 (1975): 20-24.

Brockie, Melvin D. "Full Employment, Growth and Price Stabilization." Zeitschrift des Institut fur Weltwirtschaft an der Universitat Kiel, no. 1, 1965.

Broehl, W. G., Jr. "Trade Unions and Full Employment." Southern Economic Journal 20 (1953): 61-73.

Burns, Arthur F. "Economics and Our Public Policy of Full Employment." Morgan Guaranty Survey, July 1963, pp. 4-15.

_____. "Some Reflections on the Employment Act." American Statistician 16, no. 5 (1962): 10-18.

Cahill, Faymond F. X. "Full Employment and Economic Progress: A 15-year Old Policy." Social Order 11 (1961): 457-64.

Campbell, A. D., and Jack, D. T. "Can Britain Maintain Full Employment?" Scottish Bankers Magazine 43, no. 169 (1951): 5-34.

Carter, L. H. "The Employment Act of 1946 Rejuvenated" Atlanta Economic Review 16, no. 10 (1966): 2-5.

Carver, Thomas Nixon. "The Full Employment Act of 1945." Economic Sentinel 3, no. 2 (1945): 1-64.

Chaikin, Sol C. "Boldness Will Pay Off." Viewpoint 5, no. 2 (1975): 9-15.

Chester, T. E., and Prichard, T. A. "Full Employment: Its Effect on Management Practice." Manager 21 (1953): 726ff.

Clark, Cohen. "The Economics of Overexploitation." Science, August 17, 1973.

Cohn, Jules. "The New Business of Business: A Study of a Corporate Program for the Disadvantaged." Urban Affairs Quarterly 6 (1970): 71-87.

Colm, Gerhard. "Government's Role in a Free Economy: Employment Act of 1946." Challenge 11, no. 12 (1962): 11-14.

Cooper, W. W. "Some Implications of a Program for Full Employment and Economic Stability." Political Science Quarterly 63 (1948): 230-56.

Costello, Mary. "Underemployment in America." Editorial Research Reports 11 (1975): 505-21.

Cullity, John P. "The Difficulty of Achieving the Full Employment Goal." Review of Social Economy 23 (1965): 154-63.

Dale, Ernest. "Guaranteed Wages and Employment." Southwestern Social Science Quarterly 29 (1948): 49-66.

Diamond, Irma. "The Liberation of Women in a Full Employment Society." Annals of the American Academy of Political and Social Science 418 (1975): 138-46.

Eberly, Donald J. "A National Service Pilot Project." Teachers
College Record 73, no. 1 (1971).

Eby, Kermit. "Labor's Road to Full Employment." Social Action
9, no. 10 (1945): 4-14.

Eden, Philip. "What is Full Employment?" Monthly Review 14
(1962): 309-17.

Federal Reserve Bank of Chicago. "Full Employment: Comparison
of Estimates—Views Conflict on Its Meaning and Maintenance."
Federal Reserve Bank of Chicago Business Conditions, October
1946, pp. 1-7.

Federal Reserve Bank of New York. "Full Employment and Stable
Prices." Federal Reserve Bank of New York Monthly Review 35
(1953): 156-60.

Flaim, Paul O. "Discouraged Workers and Changes in Unemployment." Monthly Labor Review 96, no. 3 (1973): 8-16.

Flanders, Ralph. "A Management View of the Road to Full Employment." Social Action 9, no. 10 (1945): 15-22.

Forsey, Eugene A. "Investment for Full Employment." Canadian
Labour 6, no. 12 (1961): 11-14.

Friedman, Milton. "The Role of Monetary Policy." American
Economic Review 58 (1968): 1-17.

"Full Employment: History and Development of the Phrase."
Statistics, December 17, 1949; January 28, and February 11,
1950 (continuing series).

"Full Employment is the Answer: An Interview with Congressman
Augustus F. Hawkins." Adherent 2, no. 2 (1975): 6-19.

Furstenberg, Frank F., Jr., and Thrall, Charles A. "Counting the
Jobless: The Impact of Job Rationing on the Measurement of
Unemployment." Annals of the American Academy of Political
and Social Science 418 (1975): 45-59.

Galbraith, John Kenneth. "The Economics of the American House-
wife." Atlantic, August 1973, pp. 78-83.

_____. "Solving Unemployment Without Inflation." Social Policy
5, no. 3 (1974): 4-5.

Gellner, Christopher G. "Enlarging the Concept of a Labor Reserve."
Monthly Labor Review 98, no. 4 (1975): 20-28.

George, E. B. "Should Full Employment Be Guaranteed?" [three
part series]. Duns Review 55, no. 2234 (1947): 17ff; 55, no. 2235
(1947): 20ff; and 55, no. 2236 (1947): 18ff.

Gilpatrick, Eleanor. "Education for Work: A Full Employment
Strategy." Annals of the American Academy of Political and
Social Science 418 (1975): 147-55.

Ginsburg, Helen. "Needed: A National Commitment to Full Employment." Current History 65 (1973): 71ff.

Gordon, Robert J. "The Welfare Cost of Higher Unemployment."
Brookings Papers on Economic Activity, no. 3 (1973): 133-205.

Gould, Julius. "Full Employment: A Discussion of Some Recent
Literature." British Journal of Sociology 3 (1952): 178-82.

Gragg, Charles I., and Teele, Stanley F. "The Proposed Full Employment Act." Harvard Business Review 23 (1945): 323-37.

Graham, Benjamin. "Some Structural Relationships Bearing Upon
Full Employment." Analysts Journal 11, no. 2 (1955): 13-16.

Graham, Frank D. "Full Employment Without Public Works, Without
Taxation, Without Public Debt, and Without Inflation." International Postwar Problems 2 (1945): 470-98.

Gross, Bertram M. "New Look for the Employment Act [of 1946]:
Five Strategic Principles." Challenge 11, no. 5 (1963): 10-13.

Gross, Bertram M., and Moses, Stanley. "Measuring the Real Work
Force: 25 Million Unemployed." Social Policy 3, no. 3 (1972):
5-10.

Gross, Bertram M., and Straussman, Jeffrey D. " 'Full' Employment
Growthmanship and the Expansion of Labor Supply." Annals of
the American Academy of Political and Social Science 418 (1975):
1-12.

Gurley, J. G. "Fiscal Policies for Full Employment: A Diagrammatic Analysis." Journal of Political Economy 60 (1952): 525-33.

Halasi, Albert. "Toward a Full Employment Program." International Postwar Problems 2 (1945): 429-62.

Hawkins, Augustus F. "Planning for Personal Choice: The Equal Opportunity and Full Employment Act." Annals of the American Academy of Political and Social Science 418 (1975): 1-12.

Hitch, T. K. "Meaning and Measurement of 'Full' or 'Maximum' Employment." Review of Economics and Statistics 33 (1951): 1-11.

Howenstine, E. J. "The Alleged Inflexibility of Compensatory Public Works Policy in the Development of Employment Policy, With Reference to United States Policy in the 1930's." Journal of Political Economy 59 (1951): 233-41.

_____. "Full Employment: A Great American Tradition." Antioch Review 6 (1946): 99-108.

_____. "Public Works Policy in the Twenties." Social Research 13 (1946): 479-500.

Hudson, Barclay M., and Sullivan, Flora. "Limited Growth, Problems of Full Employment, and the Viciousness of Easy Solutions." Socio-Economic Planning Sciences 8 (1974): 113-22.

Humphrey, Hubert H. "Guaranteed Jobs for Human Rights." Annals of the American Academy of Political and Social Science 418 (1975): 17-25.

Jackson, Henry M. "Full Employment: The Key to All Goals." American Federationist 78, no. 8 (1971): 16-18.

Jacoby, N. H. "Can Full Employment Be Achieved Without Inflation?" Commercial and Financial Chronicle, March 24, 1955, p. 12.

"Jobs for All: Any Time Soon? The Battle is On Again Over How to Achieve 'Full Employment'." U.S. News and World Report, August 2, 1971.

Jones, Byrd L. "The Role of Keynesians in Wartime Policy and Postwar Planning, 1940-46." American Economic Review 62, no. 2 (1972): 125-33.

Jones, Thomas Paine. "Full Employment and Stable Prices: The
    Economic Issues for '76." Antitrust Law and Economics Review
    7, no. 3 (1975): 5-20.

Jordan, Vernon E., Jr. "Full Employment or Depression?" Adherent
    2, no. 2 (1975): 20-25.

Joseph, Margaret F. W. "Principles of Full Employment." Inter-
    national Postwar Problems 2 (1945): 463-69.

Kapp, K. William. "Socio-Economic Effects of Low and High Employ-
    ment." Annals of the American Academy of Political and Social
    Science 418 (1975): 60-71.

Keyserling, Leon H. "For a Full Employment Act by 1976." Chal-
    lenge 18, no. 3 (1975): 22-35.

_____. "Responsibilities of Government Under the Employment
    Act of 1946." Commercial and Financial Chronicle, March 3,
    1955, p. 19.

_____. "To Procrastinate or To Plan." Viewpoint 5, no. 2 (1975):
    2-8.

Killingsworth, Charles. "Full Employment and the New Economics."
    Scottish Journal of Political Economy 16 (1969): 1-19.

_____. "Structural Unemployment in the United States" in Em-
    ployment Problems of Automation and Advanced Technology.
    Edited by Jack Steiber. New York: St. Martin's Press, 1966.

Kolberg, William H. "Employment Security Programs and the
    Economy." Labor Law Journal 25 (1974): 659-65.

Kreps, Juanita. "The Value of Women's Work" in Sex in the Market-
    place: American Women at Work. Baltimore and London: Johns
    Hopkins Press, 1973.

Kurihara, K. K. "The United Nations and Full Employment." Journal
    of Political Economy 58 (1950): 353-58.

Lando, Mordechai E. "Full Employment and the New Economics."
    Scottish Journal of Political Economy 17 (1970): 91-93.

Lebergott, Stanley. "Shall We Guarantee Full Employment?" Harper's, February 1945, pp. 193-202.

Lekachman, Robert. "Managing Inflation in a Full Employment Society." Annals of the American Academy of Political and Social Science 418 (1975): 85-93.

Lerman, Robert I. "The Public Employment Bandwagon Takes the Wrong Road." Challenge 17, no. 6 (1975): 10-16.

Lerner, Abba P. "An Integrated Full Employment Policy." International Postwar Problems 3 (1946): 69-129.

Lesser, Leonard. "Full Employment Means More Than Jobs." Viewpoint 5, no. 2 (1975): 25-28.

Levine, Morton, and Nix, James. "Guaranteed Employment and Wages Under Collective Agreements." Monthly Labor Review 74 (1952): 555-59.

Levinson, Andrew. "The Working Class Majority." New Yorker, September 2, 1974.

Levitan, Sar A. "The Emergency Employment Act: A Progress Report." Conference Board Record 9, no. 9 (1972): 46-49.

_____. "Reducing Worktime as a Means to Combat Unemployment." Upjohn Institute Public Policy Information Bulletin, September 1964.

_____. "Structural Unemployment and Public Policy." Labor Law Journal 12 (1961): 573-82.

Levitan, Sar A., and Taggert, III, Robert. "Employment and Earnings Inadequacy: A Measure of Worker Welfare." Monthly Labor Review, October 1973.

Levy, Michael E. "Full Employment Without Inflation: An Analysis of U.S. 'Phillips Curves' and 'Target' Unemployment Rates." Conference Board Record 4, no. 11 (1967): 36-41.

Livingston, David. "Labor Unions and Full Employment." Annals of the American Academy of Political and Social Science 418 (1975): 122-26.

Long, Clarence D. "Full Employment By 1963?" Challenge 10, no. 5 (1962): 10-13.

Lumer, Hyman. "Is Full Employment Possible?" Public Affairs, November 1961.

McCarthy, P. J. "Employment Policies and the Employment Act [of 1946]. " Review of Social Economy 7, no. 2 (1949): 29-33.

McCulloch, Frank W. "The Churches and Full Employment." Social Action 9, no. 10 (1945): 23-34.

McMillan, Robert A. "A Reexamination of the 'Full Employment' Goal." Federal Reserve Bank of Cleveland Economic Review, March/April 1973.

McNess, Stephen K. "The Path to Full Employment." New England Economic Review, May/June 1972, pp. 11-19.

Mangum, Garth L. "Cybernation and Job Security: The Real Culprit in Job Displacement Has Been the Slowness of Economic Growth, Not Automation." Labor Law Journal 17 (1966): 18-25.

"The Measurement of Underemployment." International Labour Review 76 (1957): 349-66.

Merry, D. H., and Bruns, G. R. "Full Employment: The British, Canadian, and Australian White Papers." Economic Record 21 (1945): 223-35.

Mikardo, Ian. "Trade Unions in a Full Employment Economy: Changed Power Relationships Between the Government and the Trade Union Movement" in New Fabian Essays. Edited by R. H. S. Crossman. London, 1952.

Mitchell, Broadus. "Full Employment and Foreign Trade." International Postwar Problems 3 (1946): 51-58.

Morton, W. A. "Trade Unionism, Full Employment, and Inflation." American Economic Review 40 (1950): 13-39.

Moses, Stanley, ed. "Planning for Full Employment." Annals of the American Academy of Political and Social Science 418 (1975): 1-165.

Moses, Stanley. "Labor Supply Concepts: The Political Economy of Conceptual Change." Annals of the American Academy of Political and Social Science 418 (1975): 26-44.

Mueller, Willard F. "Monopoly and the Inflation/Unemployment Dilemma: Trustbusting or Administrative 'Controls'?" Antitrust Law and Economics Review, Summer 1972.

Murray, James E. "Jobs for Everybody." Colliers, October 6, 1945, pp. 16ff.

Murray, James E., et. al. "Maintaining High-Level Production and Employment: A Symposium." American Political Science Review 39 (1945): 1119-79.

Nathan, Otto. "Private Enterprise and Full Employment [An Analysis of the United Nations Report on Full Employment]." Science and Society 15 (1951): 232-61.

Nathan, Robert R. "The Road to Full Employment." Industrial Relations 2, no. 1 (1962): 29-38.

National Planning Association. "The Employment Act: Twenty Years' Experience and the Future." Looking Ahead 14, no. 1 (1966): 1ff.

Newark, John. "Local Initiatives Program, 1972-1973." Canadian Manpower Review, Third Quarter, 1973.

Newman, Herbert E. "Full Employment as a Goal of Public Policy." American Journal of Economics and Sociology 17 (1958): 237-48.

Nixon, Russell, et. al. "How Much Unemployment?: A Symposium." Review of Economics and Statistics 32 (1950): 49-79.

Nourse, Edwin G. "Defining Our Government Under the 1946 Act." Review of Economics and Statistics 38 (1956): 193-204.

_____. "Early Flowering of the Employment Act of 1946." Virginia Quarterly Review 43 (1967): 233-47.

_____. "The Employment Act of 1946 and the 'New Economics'." Virginia Quarterly Review 45 (1969): 595-612.

_____. "In Pursuit of the Goals of the Employment Act: A Program for Full Employment Without Inflation." Challenge 8, no. 7 (1960): 12-17.

Nourse, Edwin G., et. al. "The Employment Act of 1946 in the Eco-
    nomic Thinking of Our Times: A Symposium." American
    Economic Review 47, no. 2 (1957): 96-144.

Odhner, Clas Erik, and Tlili, Ahmed. "Full Employment and Eco-
    nomic Development." Economic and Social Bulletin 10, no. 5
    (1962): 2-35.

O'Mahoney, J. C. "Government, Business, and the Employment Act
    of 1946: A Study of the Objectives of the Employment Act and of
    the Machinery Established for Carrying Them Out." Duns Re-
    view 57, no. 2254 (1949): 12ff.

O'Neill, David M. "Against a Federal Guaranteed Employment Pro-
    gram." Current History 65 (1973): 76ff.

O'Toole, James. "Planning for Total Employment." Annals of the
    American Academy of Political and Social Science 418 (1975):
    72-84.

_____. "The Reserve Army of the Underemployed." Change 7,
    no. 5 (1975): 26ff.

Oxenfeldt, A. R., and Van Den Baag, Ernest. "Unemployment in
    Planned and Capitalist Economies." Quarterly Journal of Eco-
    nomics 48 (1954): 43-60.

Packer, Arnold H. "Employment Guarantees Should Replace the Wel-
    fare System." Challenge 17, no. 1 (1974): 21-27.

Packer, Stephen B. "What Do We Know About A Full Employment
    Budget?" Challenge 12, no. 10 (1964): 35-37.

Patinkin, Donald. "Price Flexibility and Full Employment." Ameri-
    can Economic Review 38 (1948): 543-64.

Patton, J. G. "Full Employment: A Proposal [National Farm Union's
    Proposed 'Full Employment Act of 1950']." Antioch Review 8
    (1948): 417-24.

Pearl, Arthur, and Pearl, Stephanie. "Strategies for Radical Social
    Change: Toward an Ecological Theory of Value." Social Policy
    2, no. 1 (1971): 30ff.

Perry, George L. "Changing Labor Markets and Inflation." Brook-
    ings Papers on Economic Activity, no. 3 (1971): 533-78.

Phelps, Edmund S. "Unreasonable Price Stability: The Pyrrhic Victory Over Inflation" in The Battle Against Unemployment. Edited by Arthur M. Okun. New York: W. W. Norton, 1972.

Phillips, A. W. "The Relation Between Unemployment and the Rate of Change of Money Wage Rates in the United Kingdom, 1862-1957." Economica 25 (1958): 283-99.

Pierson, John H. G. "National Budget as an Aid in Reducing Deficits Under Assured Full Employment." Monthly Labor Review 61 (1945): 210-14.

_____. "The Underwriting Approach to Full Employment: A Further Explanation." Review of Economics and Statistics 31 (1949): 182-92.

Pleeter, Saul. "Will Public Service Employment Do the Job?" Business Horizons 18, no. 2 (1975): 41-47.

Poole, William. "Alternative Paths to a Stable Full Employment Economy." Brookings Papers on Economic Activity, no. 3, 1971.

Rees, Albert. "Collective Bargaining, Full Employment and Inflation" in Proceedings of the Annual Conference of McGill University Industrial Relations Centre, 1953. Montreal: McGill University, 1953.

Rees, A. E. "Wage Levels Under Conditions of Long-Run Full Employment." American Economic Review 43, no. 2 (1953): 451-57.

Ruml, Beardsley. "Financing Postwar Prosperity: Controlling Booms and Depressions." Vital Speeches 10 (1943): 95-96.

Schweitzer, Stuart O., and Smith, Ralph E. "The Persistence of the Discouraged Worker Effect." Industrial and Labor Relations Review 27 (1974): 249-60.

Shanahan, Eileen. "The Mystery of the Great Calm of the Unemployed." New York Times, August 3, 1975.

Shapiro, David L. "Is Inflation Necessary for Full Employment?" Arizona Business Bulletin 17, no. 4 (1970): 3-11.

Shragge, Eric. "Community Employment Programs: Relief, Regulation, or Service to People?" Canadian Welfare 51, no. 2 (1975): 22-24.

Singer, Morris. "Inflation Without Full Employment: A Case Study." Social Research 26 (1959): 1-17.

Solow, Robert M. "A Policy for Full Employment." Industrial Relations 2, no. 1 (1962): 1-14.

_____. "What Happened to Full Employment?" Quarterly Review of Economics and Business 13, no. 2 (1973): 7-20.

Sonne, H. Christian. "The Employment Act: 1946-1961." Looking Ahead, February 1961.

Spring, William. "Underemployment: The Measure We Refuse To Take." New Generation 53, no. 1 (1971): 20-25.

Spring, William; Harrison, Bennett; and Vietorisz, Thomas. "Crisis of the Underemployed." New York Times Magazine, November 5, 1972.

Stevens, Morris L. "Is Full Employment Possible Without Inflation?" Midwest Quarterly 1 (1960): 163-82.

Sultan, P. E. "Social Pressures, Stability, and Full Employment." American Journal of Economics and Sociology 13 (1954): 159-70.

Tabush, Victor. "Underemployment." Arizona Review 24, no. 4 (1975): 9-12.

Thomas, R. D. "Economics and Full Employment." Southwestern Social Science Quarterly 27 (1947): 345-62.

Thurow, Lester C. "Redistributional Aspects of Manpower Training Programs" in Manpower Programs in the Policy Mix. Edited by Lloyd Ulman. Baltimore: Johns Hopkins University Press, 1973.

Tobin, James. "Inflation and Unemployment." American Economic Review 62 (1972): 1-18.

Tucker, James F. "The Employment Act of 1946: A Review of Postwar Public Policy on Employment." Atlanta Economic Review 24, no. 2 (1974): 22-27.

Ulmer, Melville, J. "Full Employment Without Inflation." Social Policy 5, no. 5 (1975): 7-12.

_____ . "Things You Never Knew About Unemployment." New Republic, May 6, 1972, pp. 14ff.

"Unemployment and Full Employment: Discussions at the General Assembly of the United Nations—Resolutions Concerning Full Employment." Industry and Labour 3 (1950): 52-60.

U.S. Council of Economic Advisors. "The Employment Act: Twenty Years of Experience" in Manpower Problems and Policies. Edited by John A. Delehanty. Scranton, Pa.: International Textbook Co., 1969.

"U.S. Employment Policy [submitted to Congress by President Truman in his first annual economic report under the Employment Act of 1946]." International Labour Review 55 (1947): 123-24.

Van Leesten, Michael S. "Bottoming Out or Lifting Up: A Case for Full Employment." Adherent 2, no. 2 (1975): 26-28.

Vietorisz, Thomas, et. al. "Subemployment: Exclusion and Inadequacy Indexes." Monthly Labor Review 98, no. 5 (1975): 3-12.

Vietorisz, Thomas; Mier, Robert; and Harrison, Bennett. "Full Employment at Living Wages." Annals of the American Academy of Political and Social Science 418 (1975): 94-107.

Viner, Jacob. "Full Employment at Whatever Cost: Analysis of United Nations Report on Full Employment." Quarterly Journal of Economics 64 (1950): 385-407.

Von Mises, Ludwig. "Full Employment and Monetary Policy: Are Labor Unions Desirable?" National Review 3 (1957): 589-91.

Wallich, H. C. "United Nations Report on Full Employment: Comment." American Economic Review 40 (1950): 876-83.

Warner, David C. "Fiscal Barriers to Full Employment." Annals of the American Academy of Political and Social Science 418 (1975): 156-64.

Wasserman, William S., and Lutz, Harley L. "Should Government Guarantee Employment?" Modern Industry, June 15, 1945.

Watson, Thomas J., et. al. "Unemployment: The Spectre that Haunts the West." Realities, February 1964.

Weintraub, E. Roy, and Weintraub, Sidney. "The Full Employment Model: A Critique." Kyklos 25 (1972): 83-100.

Wheildon, L. B. "Guarantee of Wages and Employment." Editorial Research Reports 1 (1947): 417-33.

Wickendon, Elizabeth. "A Guaranteed Income: Supplement to Full Employment Guarantees." Annals of the American Academy of Political and Social Science 418 (1975): 108-21.

Williams, Harrison, and Vorys, John. "Can We Have Full Employment With Freer Trade?" Town Meeting, February 23, 1954.

Wilson, R. E. "Industry's Responsibility for Job Creation and Job Security." Commercial and Financial Chronicle, June 23, 1955, p. 13.

GOVERNMENT DOCUMENTS

U.S., Congress, House, Committee on Banking and Currency. Area Assistance Act of 1956: Hearings, April 12-26, 1954 on H.R. 555. 84th Cong., 2nd sess., 1956.

U.S., Congress, House, Committee on Education and Labor, Select Subcommittee on Labor. Emergency Employment Act of 1971: Hearings, February 24-March 17, 1971. 92nd Cong., 1st sess., 1971.

_____. The Emergency Jobs Act of 1974: Hearings, October 1-10, 1974 on H.R. 16596. 93rd Cong., 2nd sess., 1974.

_____. Public Service Employment: Hearings, May 7 through July 1, 1968 on H.R. 12280 and Other Bills. 90th Cong., 2nd sess., 1968.

U.S., Congress, House, Committee on Education and Labor, Subcommittee on Equal Opportunities. Equal Opportunity and Full Employment Act of 1976: Hearings on H.R. 15476. 93rd Cong., 1st sess., 1975.

_____. Equal Opportunity and Full Employment Act: Hearings on H.R. 50, Parts I, II, III, and IV. 94th Cong., 1st sess., 1975.

U.S., Congress, House, Committee on Public Works. Public Works and Economic Development Act of 1965: Hearings on H.R. 6991, May 10-26, 1965. 89th Cong., 1st sess., 1965.

U.S., Congress, House, Committee on Ways and Means. The Work Incentive Program: First Annual Report of the Department of Labor. 91st Cong., 2nd sess., 1970.

U.S., Congress, House, Committee on Ways and Means, Subcommittee on Health. Health Insurance for the Unemployed and Related Legislation: Hearings, March 3-10, 1975. 94th Cong., 1st sess., 1975.

U.S., Congress, Joint Economic Committee. Economic Policies and Practices: Unemployment Programs in Sweden. 88th Cong., 2nd sess., 1964.

_____. Employment Act of 1964, as Amended, with Related Laws (annotated) and Rules. 90th Cong., 1st sess., 1967.

_____. Reducing Unemployment to 2 Percent: Hearings, October 17-26, 1972. 92nd Cong., 2nd sess., 1972.

_____. State of the Economy and Policies for Full Employment: Hearings, August 7-22, 1962. 87th Cong., 2nd sess., 1962.

U.S., Congress, Library of Congress, Legislative Reference Service, Economics Division. Should the Federal Government Establish a National Program of Public Work for the Unemployed?; Selected Excerpts and References Relating to the National College Debate Topic, 1964-65. Washington, D.C.: U.S. Government Printing Office, 1964.

U.S., Congress, Senate. Assuring Full Employment in a Free Competitive Economy. 79th Cong., 1st sess., Senate Report 583. Reprinted together with Minority Report in Senate Committee on Labor and Public Welfare, History of Employment and Manpower Policy in the United States. Washington, D.C.: U.S. Government Printing Office, 1965.

_____. Full Employment Act of 1945: Hearings Before a Subcommittee on Banking and Currency on S. 380. 79th Cong., 1st sess., 1945.

U.S., Congress, Senate, Committee on Banking and Currency, Subcommittee on Production and Currency. Employment Act Amendments: Hearings, February 24-26, 1960 on S. 64 and S. 2382.
86th Cong., 2nd sess., 1960.

U.S., Congress, Senate, Committee on Finance. Health Insurance and
the Unemployed: Hearing, March 7, 1975 on S. 496. 94th Cong.,
1st sess., 1975.

_____. Welfare Reform: Guaranteed Job Opportunity—Explanation
of Committee Decisions. 92nd Cong., 2nd sess., 1972.

U.S., Congress, Senate, Committee on Labor and Public Welfare.
Manpower Development and Training Act of 1961: Report, July
31, 1961, together with individual views (to accompany S. 19911).
87th Cong., 1st sess., 1961.

_____. Towards Full Employment: Proposals for a Comprehensive
Employment and Manpower Policy in the United States. 88th
Cong., 2nd sess., 1964.

U.S., Congress, Senate, Committee on Labor and Public Welfare,
Subcommittee on Employment and Manpower. Selected Readings
in Employment and Manpower, Vol. 2. 88th Cong., 2nd sess.,
1964.

_____. Selected Readings in Employment and Manpower, Vol. 5:
History of Employment and Manpower Policy in the United States:
Parts 1 and 2; Depression Experience, Proposals and Programs.
88th Cong., 2nd sess., 1964.

_____. Selected Readings in Employment and Manpower, Vol. 6:
History of Employment and Manpower Policy in the United States:
Parts 3 and 4; Looking Ahead to the Postwar Economy and the
Concept of Full Employment in Congress. 88th Cong., 2nd sess.,
1964.

_____. Selected Readings in Employment and Manpower: Vol. 7;
History of Employment and Manpower Policy in the United States;
Parts 1 and 2: Twenty Years of Experience Under the Employ-
ment Act of 1946. 89th Cong., 2nd sess., 1966.

_____. To Amend the Employment Act of 1946: Hearings, October
18-20, 1964 on S. 1630. 89th Cong., 1st sess., 1965.

U.S., Congress, Senate, Committee on Labor and Public Welfare, Subcommittee on Employment, Manpower, and Poverty. Case Studies of the Emergency Employment Act in Operation. 93rd Cong., 1st sess., 1973.

_____. Comprehensive Manpower Reform: Hearings, Part 5. 92nd Cong., 2nd sess., 1972.

_____. The Emergency Employment Act: An Interim Assessment. 92nd Cong., 2nd sess., 1972.

_____. The JOBS Program: Background Information. 91st Cong., 2nd sess., 1970.

U.S., Congress, Senate, Committee on Labor and Public Welfare, Subcommittee on Employment, Poverty, and Migratory Labor. Public Service Employment Legislation, 1974: Hearings, September 16 through October 17 on S. 4079. 93rd Cong., 2nd sess., 1974.

U.S., Congress, Senate, Committee on Labor and Public Welfare, Subcommittee on Labor. Hearings: January 1 through February 24, 1956 on S. 2663. 84th Cong., 2nd sess., 1956.

U.S., Congress, Senate, Committee on Public Works. Public Works and Economic Development Act of 1965: Hearings, April 26 through May 3, 1965 on S. 1648. 89th Cong., 1st sess., 1965.

U.S., Department of Labor, Bureau of Labor Statistics. How the Government Measures Unemployment. Washington, D.C.: U.S. Government Printing Office, 1973.

U.S., Department of Labor, Manpower Administration. Special Job Creation for the Hard-to-employ in Western Europe (Manpower Research Monograph no. 14). Washington, D.C.: U.S. Government Printing Office, 1970.

U.S., Department of Labor, Manpower Administration, Office of Manpower Policy, Evaluation, and Research. Report of the Secretary of Labor, 1966, on Manpower Research and Training Under the Manpower Development and Training Act of 1962. Washington, D.C.: U.S. Government Printing Office, 1966.

U.S., Equal Employment Opportunity Commission. Toward Fair Employment and the E.E.O.C. Washington, D.C.: U.S. Government Printing Office, 1973.

U.S., Federal Reserve Board of Governors. Public Finance and Full Employment. Washington, D.C.: U.S. Government Printing Office, December 1945.

PAMPHLETS AND OTHER DOCUMENTS

American Federation of Labor, Industrial Union Department. What Everyone Should Know About Government Spending and Full Employment. (Publication No. 53). Washington, D.C.: AFL-CIO, 1963.

Citizens National Committee. Full Employment and the National Budget. (Research Report No. 2-417). Washington, D.C.: Citizens National Committee, 1945.

Citizens Research Bureau. What the People Think About Full Employment. Chicago: Citizens Research Bureau, 1945.

Clark, Harrison. Swedish Unemployment Policy—1914 to 1940. Washington, D.C.: American Council on Public Affairs, n.d.

Conference on Economic Progress. Key Policies for Full Employment. Washington, D.C.: Conference on Economic Progress, September 1962.

_____. Toward Full Employment and Full Production: How To End Our National Economic Deficits. Washington, D.C.: Conference on Economic Progress, July 1954.

Congress of Industrial Organizations, Political Action Committee. Four Men Speak About Jobs for All. New York: CIO Political Action Committee, 1944.

Council of Europe, Secretariat-General. Full Employment Objectives in Relation to the Problem of European Cooperation. Strasbourg: Council of Europe, 1951.

Couturier, Jean J. Government as Employer of First Resort. (speech before the annual meeting of the American Society of Public Administration). March 1972. Mimeographed.

Easterbrook, Frank H. Public Employment Programs: A Selected and Annotated Bibliography; O.E.O. Working Papers, Series

3250, no. 2. Washington, D.C.: Office of Economic Opportunity, November 1970. Mimeographed.

Fechter, Alan. Public Employment Programs: Evaluative Study No. 20. Washington, D.C.: American Enterprise Institute, 1975.

Gaer, Joseph, and Lamb, Robert K. The Answer Is Full Employment. (Pamphlet of the Month No. 4). New York: CIO Political Action Committee, 1945.

Goble, Frank G. Towards 100% Employment: An American Management Association Survey Report. New York: American Management Association, 1973.

Great Britain, Treasury. Must Full Employment Mean Ever-Rising Prices? London: Her Majesty's Stationers, 1956.

Hazlitt, Henry. Implications of State Guarantee of Employment. New York: Academy of Political Science, Columbia University, 1945. Mimeographed.

Higgins, Benjamin Howard. Public Investment and Full Employment. Montreal: International Labour Office, 1946.

Holt, Charles C., et. al. The Unemployment/Inflation Dilemma: A Manpower Solution. Washington, D.C.: The Urban Institute, 1971.

Industrial Relations Counselors, Inc. Manpower and Planning. New York: Industrial Relations Counselors, Inc., 1970.

Institute for Local Self-Government. Proceedings of the Western Workshop on Public Employment and the Disadvantaged. Berkeley, Calif.: Institute for Local Self-Government, 1970.

International Labour Office, Geneva. Unemployment and Public Works. Geneva: International Labour Office, 1931.

Keyserling, Leon. Full Employment Without Inflation. Washington, D.C.: Conference on Economic Progress, 1975.

Lekachman, Robert. Public Service Employment: Jobs for All. (Public Affairs pamphlet no. 481). New York: Public Affairs Committee, Inc., 1972.

League of Nations Union of Great Britain. Conference on Unemployment, London, 1924. Geneva: International Labour Office, 1924.

Moore, Geoffrey. How Full is Full Employment? Washington, D.C.: American Enterprise Institute, 1973.

National Commission for Manpower Policy. Proceedings of a Conference on Public Service Employment. Washington, D.C.: National Manpower Policy Task Force, 1974.

National Manpower Policy Task Force. Adapting Labor Market Statistics to Policy Needs: A Policy Statement. Washington, D.C.: National Policy Task Force, 1974.

National Planning Association. An Evaluation of the Economic Impact Project of the Public Employment Program. Washington, D.C.: National Planning Association, May 1974.

_____. National Budgets for Full Employment. (Planning pamphlets nos. 43 and 44). Washington, D.C.: National Planning Association, 1945.

New York State Department of Labor, Division of Research and Statistics. Guaranteed Annual Employment, New York State, 1955. Albany, N.Y.: New York State Department of Labor, June 1956.

Organization for Economic Cooperation and Development. International Conference on Employment Fluctuations and Manpower Policy, London, 1969. Paris: Manpower and Social Affairs Directorat, OECD, 1971.

_____. International Management Seminar on Active Manpower Policy, Brussels, 1964. Paris: Manpower and Social Affairs Directorat, OECD, 1965.

Pierson, John H. G. Fiscal Policy for Full Employment. (Planning pamphlet no. 45). Washington, D.C.: National Planning Association, 1945.

Schmidt, Emerson P. Can Government Guarantee Full Employment? (Postwar Readjustments Bulletin no. 13). Washington, D.C.: U.S. Chamber of Commerce, 1945.

_____. Full Employment, Its Politics and Economics. (Postwar Readjustments Bulletin no. 9). Washington, D.C.: U.S. Chamber of Commerce, 1944.

Spates, Thomas Gardner. International Planning of Public Works: A Factor in the Regularization of Employment and Economic Relationships. Geneva: Geneva Research Center, 1932.

The Times, London. Full Employment: Ten Articles Reprinted from the London Times. London: The Times Publishing Co., 1943.

United Nations, Economic and Social Council. Full Employment: Measures to Prevent Possible Inflation at High Levels of Economic Activity. (Resolution no. 483A). New York: United Nations, April 22, 1954.

_____. World Economic Trends: Report on Activities in Relation to Full Employment Objectives. New York: United Nations, July 3, 1962.

United Nations. National and International Measures for Full Employment. (UN Document E15844-22). Lake Success, N.Y.: United Nations, December 1949.

United Nations Secretariat, Department of Economic Affairs. Implementation of Full Employment Policies, Report No. 1. (UN Document No. ST/ECA/5, July 6, 1950). Lake Success, N.Y.: United Nations, 1950.

_____. Maintenance of Full Employment. Lake Success, N.Y.: United Nations, 1949.

_____. Problems of Unemployment and Inflation. (UN Document No. E/2035/rev. 1. ST/ECA/12, August 2, 1951.). New York: United Nations, 1951.

Upjohn Institute for Community Research. Full Employment in Your Community: A Report by Samuel V. Bennett, et. al. Chicago: Public Administration Service, 1947.

Woodcock, Leonard. Keynote Address at the Founding Meeting of the National Committee for Full Employment, June 14, 1974. New York: National Conference on Public Service Employment, 1974. Mimeographed.

MISCELLANEOUS

Ashbrook, Arthur G., Jr. "Federal Wage-Price Policy for a Full Employment Economy." Ph.D. dissertation, Massachusetts Institute of Technology, 1948.

Bailey, Stephen K. "The Politics of Full Employment: A Study in the Formulation of Public Policy." Ph.D. dissertation, Harvard University, 1948.

Brannon, Gerard M. "The Problem of National Income Prediction Errors in Full Employment Policy." Ph.D. dissertation, Harvard University, 1950.

Campbell, Rita R. "Annual Wage and Employment Guarantee Plans." Ph.D. dissertation, Radcliffe College, 1947.

District 65 v. Richard M. Nixon, et. al., 72-1778 SDNY (1972).

Fisher, Louis, Jr. "Full Employment and the Constitution; A Study in Presidential Economics." Ph.D. dissertation, New School for Social Research, 1967.

Glenn, Lowell Marshall. "Public Service Employment for the Disadvantaged." Ph.D. dissertation, George Washington University, 1974.

Hagelin, Edith Hilma. "The Swedish Full Employment Policy and Economic Development, 1945-1952." Ph.D. dissertation, Harvard University, 1964.

Hogg, Malcolm W. "Full Employment Policies and International Equilibrium." Ph.D. dissertation, University of Chicago, 1950.

Lewis, John P. "Toward an Administrable Price Policy for Full Employment." Ph.D. dissertation, Harvard University, 1950.

Margolis, Julius. "The Economic Effects of Counter-Cyclical Public Works Programming." Ph.D. dissertation, Harvard University, 1949.

Meany, George. "Address Before the Full Employment Action Council." Washington, D.C.: June 17, 1975. Mimeographed.

Moore, Carl Marcus. "The Issues, Strategies and Structure of the
    Senate Debate Over the Full Employment Bill of 1945." Ph.D.
    dissertation, Wayne State University, 1972.

Patrick, John David. "The Balance of Payments, Full Employment,
    and Growth: A Study of the Convergence and Consistency of Inter-
    national Economic Policy." Ph.D. dissertation, Columbia Univer-
    sity, 1969.

Peppers, Larry Craig. "The Full Employment Surplus in the 1930's."
    Ph.D. dissertation, Vanderbilt University, 1970.

Plous, Harold J. "The Hazards of Full Employment." Ph.D. disserta-
    tion, University of Wisconsin, 1951.

Reuther, Walter P. "Full Employment: Key to Abundance, Security,
    Peace." (Address before the UAW-CIO Conference on Full Em-
    ployment, Washington, D.C., December 6-7, 1953.) Mimeographed.

Schlender, William Elmer. "An Investigation of Certain Basic Manage-
    ment Problems Under Annual Guarantees of Employment and
    Wages." Ph.D. dissertation, Ohio State University, 1955.

Seastone, Don A. "Guaranteed Wages and Employment and Their Role
    in Collective Bargaining." Ph.D. dissertation, University of
    Oregon, 1954.

Somers, Gerald G. "The Significance of Trade Unionism in the In-
    flationary Potential of Full Employment." Ph.D. dissertation,
    University of California at Berkeley, 1951.

Wagner, Ludwig Anton. "The Wage Policy of the Swedish Trade
    Unions Under Full Employment and Full Unionization." Ph.D.
    dissertation, Columbia University, 1955.

White, Sammis Brownell. "The Potential of Subsidized Job Creation
    in Reducing Employment Deprivations During a Period of Full
    Aggregate Employment." Ph.D. dissertation, University of
    Pennsylvania, 1971.

Wittich, Gunter Johann. "The German Road to Full Employment."
    Ph.D. dissertation, University of California at Berkeley, 1966.

ABOUT THE EDITORS AND CONTRIBUTORS

ALAN GARTNER is Codirector of the New Human Services Institute at Queens College, City University of New York. He is Secretary of the National Conference on Public Service Employment and Publisher of Social Policy Magazine. Mr. Gartner is the author of Paraprofessionals and Their Performance and coauthor of The Service Society and the Consumer Vanguard.

He received his A.B. from Antioch College, his M.A. from Harvard University, and his Ph.D. from the Union Graduate School, Union of Experimenting Colleges and Universities.

WILLIAM LYNCH, JR. is Director of Training, New Careers Training Laboratory, Queens College. He is Executive Director of the National Conference on Public Service Employment.

FRANK RIESSMAN is Codirector of the New Human Services Institute, Queens College, and Editor of Social Policy Magazine. Mr. Riessman is the author of several books, including The Culturally Deprived Child and Strategies Against Poverty, and coauthor of The Service Society and the Consumer Vanguard.

He received his A.B. from City College, his M.A. from Columbia University, and his Ph.D. from Columbia University.

RUSSELL A. NIXON, who died in 1973, was Professor of Social Policy and Social Welfare in the School of Social Work, Columbia University.

BERTRAM A. GROSS is Distinguished Professor of Urban Affairs and Planning, Hunter College of the City University of New York.

CHARLES C. KILLINGSWORTH is University Professor of Economics, Labor, and Industrial Relations at Michigan State University.

EMILE BENOIT is a professor in the Columbia University Schools of Business and International Affairs.

ROBERT LEKACHMAN is Distinguished Professor of Economics at Herbert H. Lehman College of the City University of New York.

BENNETT HARRISON is Associate Professor of Economics and Urban Studies in the Department of Urban Studies and Planning at the Massachusetts Institute of Technology.

LEON H. KEYSERLING, a consulting economist and attorney, is President of the Conference on Economic Progress.

DEPRIVED URBAN YOUTH: An Economic and
Cross-Cultural Analysis of the United States,
Colombia, and Peru
> John P. Walter, William H. Leahy, and
> Arthur G. Dobbelaere

HIGH LEVEL MANPOWER AND TECHNOLOGI-
CAL CHANGE IN THE STEEL INDUSTRY: Implications for Corporate Manpower Planning
> Dale L. Hiestand
> foreword by Eli Ginzberg

THE SCOPE OF BARGAINING IN PUBLIC EM-
PLOYMENT
> Joan Weitzman

THE URBAN LABOR MARKET: Institutions, Information, Linkages
> David Lewin, Raymond Horton,
> Robert Shick, and Charles Brecher
> foreword by Eli Ginzberg

WOMEN IN ACADEMIA: Evolving Policies Toward Equal Opportunities
> edited by Elga Wasserman,
> Arie Y. Lewin, and Linda H. Bleiweis

WORKER MILITANCY AND ITS CONSEQUENCES,
1965-75: New Directions in Western Industrial
Relations*
> edited by Solomon Barkin

*Also available in paperback as a PSS Student Edition.